BY THE AUTHOR

Novels
Surviving Sting
Kiss Me Softly, Amy Turtle
Do I Love You?

Poetry
The Right Suggestion
Catch a Falling Tortoise
An Artist Goes Bananas

Criticism
Fiction from the Furnace
Student Guide to Philip Roth
Laughing at the Darkness
Reading *Catch-22*
Reading Toni Morrison's *Beloved*

Philosophy
The Philosophy of Humour

As Editor
Loffing Matters
The Tipping Point

STORYTELLING

STORYTELLING
Narratology for Critics and Creative Writers

PAUL MCDONALD

Greenwich Exchange
London

Greenwich Exchange, London

First published in Great Britain in 2014
All rights reserved

Paul McDonald © 2014

This book is sold subject to the conditions that it shall not, by way of trade or otherwise, be lent, resold, hired out or otherwise circulated without the publisher's prior consent in any form of binding or cover other than that in which it is published and without a similar condition including this condition being imposed on the subsequent purchaser.

Printed and bound by imprintdigital.net
Cover design by Maurice Burns

Greenwich Exchange Website: www.greenex.co.uk

Cataloguing in Publication Data is available from the British Library

Cover art: Clive Watts 'Ringer #1'
(reproduced courtesy of Shutterstock Inc)

ISBN: 978-1-906075-90-3

CONTENTS

Introduction *11*

What is a Narrative? *12*

What is Fiction? *13*

Narrative versus Story *15*

The Organisation of a Story *19*

The Deep Structure of Stories *23*

Structure for Creative Writers *30*

Who Tells the Story? *34*

Narrative Levels *35*

Focalisation *37*

First-Person Narrators *39*

Unreliable Narrators *42*

Idiosyncratic Narrators *42*

Naïve Narrators *44*

Insane Narrators *48*

First-Person Narrators of Other People's Stories *50*

First-Person Narrators and Emotional Engagement *51*

First-Person Narration and Questions of Value *53*

Third-Person Narrators *56*

Authorial Narrators *57*

Modern and Modernist Narrators *59*

Postmodern Narrators *66*

Narrative and Viewpoint Issues for Creative Writers *72*

Characters *76*

Are Fictional Characters Like People? *78*

Character or Plot? *80*

Types of Character *82*

Characterisation *85*

Direct Definition *85*

Indirect Presentation *86*

Action *87*

Speech *87*

Appearance *88*

Environment *89*

Reinforcement: Analogy and Contrast *90*

Character Issues for Creative Writers *92*

Speech in Narrative *95*

Dialogue and Creative Writing *101*

Conclusion: Creating Critical and Fictional Narratives *103*

Bibliography: Books on Narrative *107*

Useful Books for Creative Writers *110*

Fictional Narratives Mentioned *111*

Introduction

The American novelist Joan Didion said, 'We tell ourselves stories in order to live'[1], and this doesn't feel like an exaggeration: fiction is fundamental to the human experience. For the duration of recorded history people have been creating it and writing it down. Certainly, the earliest texts in existence – those written in ancient Sumer five thousand years ago – contain tales of adventure, horror, love, and humour of a kind that have much in common with the fictions of the modern world. We engage with fiction in a variety of ways, and for different reasons: for entertainment, of course, but also to achieve a deeper understanding of the world, and of ourselves. This book is for those who seek an insight into the mechanics of fiction, either because they are students of literary criticism, or aspiring creative writers. In its account of narrative techniques, it introduces some of the key issues addressed by narratologists, explaining the more useful

---

[1] She uses this as the title of her collected non-fiction works (New York: Alfred A. Knopf, 2006)

terminology and concepts, and applying them to texts that are commonly studied on literature courses. It focuses on the constituent elements of stories: their structure, the significance of who tells them, and the important aspects of characterisation and dialogue. Throughout, the aim is to make the discussions accessible, and relevant both to critics and creative writers.

What is a Narrative?

Consider this text:

> The last man on Earth sat alone in a room. There was a knock on the door ...

This is a short story called 'Knock' by the science fiction writer Fredric Brown.[2] It can be called a narrative because it relates two activities: the last man on earth sitting alone in a room, followed by a knock at the door. In other words, it presents a series of events, which take place in time – in the sense that one follows the other. Now consider this:

> Love is not a thing to understand.
> Love is not a thing to feel.
> Love is not a thing to give and receive.
> Love is a thing only to become
> And eternally be.

---

[2] This was originally published in *Thrilling Wonder Stories* (December 1948). It is actually the opening sentence of a longer story, but clearly works as a story in its own right. The longer version can be read here: http://koapp.narod.ru/english/fantast/book34.htm

This is a poem called 'Love Is a Thing to Become' by the Indian poet Sri Chinmoy.[3] It would be difficult to describe this as a narrative because there is no series of events or activities: it refers only to the supposed characteristics of an abstract concept. This book's focus will be on verbal, fictional narrative (written and oral) – so I will not spend much time discussing non-verbal narrative such as, say, ballet, or narrative that mixes words with visual images or performance such as film or drama; similarly, I'm not particularly concerned with so-called non-fiction like history, biography or journalism.

What is Fiction?

Perhaps the first point worth making about verbal narrative is that, arguably, it is all fictional. Firstly, assuming that narratives are produced by human beings, it is hard to think of them as ever being truly objective: all narratives have the potential to be influenced by the biases of their creator. Also, because they are finite and can never be fully comprehensive, they cannot tell the whole story. So, as well as being biased, narratives are, of necessity, selective and incomplete. In addition, verbal narratives use language to communicate, and language is a notoriously slippery medium. There is no fixed relationship between words and the world they represent; you cannot nail their meaning down, and you can never be sure

---

[3] Sri Chinmoy. 'Love is a thing to Become' quoted on the poet's website http://www.srichinmoypoetry.com/library/poems/love-is-a-thing-to-become/

of how they will signify to readers. In other words, it is always hard to be absolutely sure what any verbal narrative means. Thus, while they might purport to deal in reality, non-fiction narratives can only be said to convey approximations of reality; they are, as some might want to put it, fictional.

Of course, the essential difference between fiction and non-fiction is how it is perceived, and the assumptions readers hold about these categories. Once a narrative has been presented as non-fiction, this creates expectations in the reader about the nature of the material. They expect it to be true, they expect it to adhere to the facts, and authors are held accountable accordingly. One advantage that fiction has over non-fiction is that readers don't expect literal truth, and writers aren't usually answerable in quite the same way should they address controversial or sensitive issues. Such issues can be explored 'in character' in a world which is always qualified to some degree by its fictional status. The realm of fiction can be liberating, then, because it allows writers to be less circumspect than they might otherwise be; this is why it is often said that the truth is usually to be found in an author's fiction rather than their autobiographies. I have often heard people say that they don't read fiction because they don't like wasting time on things that aren't true. I would say that, as far as it's possible for any narrative to deal in truths, you're just as likely to find them in fiction as in so-called non-fiction.

Narrative versus Story

It is useful to be able to make a distinction between stories and narratives. In this book the former will refer to what is told, and the latter will refer to *how* it is told. In other words, it is assumed that a story can be abstracted from a particular narrative; a story can exist *independently* of a specific narrative. Imagine that you were thinking of writing a story with the following basic plot:

> Dave meets a stranger called Nigel in a bar one night – they have a nice chat before Dave has to leave. He drives home and sleeps soundly. Next morning Dave gets up to go to work, opens the boot of his car and finds Nigel's severed head inside.

How would you narrate a story of this kind in order to create the best effect? The most effective way might not be chronological. Some writers might want to begin with Dave's discovery of the severed head because this would offer a good dramatic opening; from then on the story could take the form of a mystery: who is Nigel and how did his head come to be in Dave's car? The reader's desire to have that mystery solved would keep them engaged. However, the story *could* also work chronologically: when Dave meets Nigel the reader will automatically wonder what the significance of that meeting is likely to be, and the anticipation of finding out will generate suspense. This may be the case in genres such as crime and horror, for instance, where readers have certain expectations about what's going to happen. Mystery and suspense are fundamental to storytelling, of course, and they are created via narrative organisation.

To illustrate this further, consider the following story:

> My girlfriend died laughing at one of my funny faces. Her friends were kind, and told me I shouldn't feel guilty; that she would have wanted to die that way. They weren't there as her musical laughter turned to chokes, grunts and her death rattle. When I stopped grieving I found a beautiful new girl to love. She died laughing at a joke I made about her feet. The next one passed away similarly. My last girlfriend didn't die. She left me. She said we never had any fun together. That she wanted a man with a sense of humour.

This very short story by Dan Rhodes is called 'Laughing'[4]. Clearly the narrative is arranged in order to convey the story in a way that makes sense; however, we can change the narrative quite radically without actually changing the essence of the story:

> My last girlfriend didn't die. She left me. She said we never had any fun together. That she wanted a man with a sense of humour. My first girlfriend died laughing at one of my funny faces. Her friends were kind, and told me I shouldn't feel guilty; that she would have wanted to die that way. They weren't there as her musical laughter turned to chokes, grunts and her death rattle. When I stopped grieving I found a beautiful new girl to love. She died laughing at a joke I made about her feet. The next one passed away similarly.

---

[4] Dan Rhodes, 'Laughing', *Pulp.Net: The Online Home of New Fiction*. November, 2008. http://www.pulp.net/49/100-words.html

In the second version the narrative has been restructured, but the story remains essentially the same. Most people would feel that the first version is better, of course, because it builds narrative tension, working its way to a climax and setting up the final line which functions like a punch line in a joke. This effect is ruined in the second version, and yet it is the same story: the speaker narrates his experiences with a series of girlfriends, all of whom died laughing apart from the most recent girlfriend who left him because she didn't find him funny. Once you have finished reading the second version you can reassemble the events of the story in the same chronological order as the first version. So this illustrates the difference between story and narrative; the latter is a vehicle for the former: a story is something that can be extracted from the narrative and expressed as a linear series of events.

For the purposes of this book, I will use the term story to refer to the events as they occur chronologically, independent of the narrative, while the term narrative will be used to refer to the telling or the organisation of the story. The fact that stories can exist – to a degree – independently of narratives is the reason why it is possible to reproduce them in different ways, via different narrative media. So, for instance, J.K. Rowling's series of Harry Potter stories exist both as novels and films; and even though those narrative worlds differ, there is a sense in which the stories stay the same. I say 'a sense in which' because it would be wrong to think that they are identical. Stories are made in the telling to a large extent, and any changes to the narrative impact on how we relate to them. However, it is clear that stories have a deep structure that can be paraphrased and retold in different ways. This is one of the ways in which stories could be said to differ from poems: the former can be paraphrased, while the latter tend to be dependent on, or inextricably bound up with, the way they are expressed.

A term that is often used in relation to stories is plot. Some critics like to make a distinction between these two things. For instance, in his classic study *Aspects of the Novel* (1927) the English novelist E.M. Forster says the following:

> We have defined story as a narrative of events arranged in a time-sequence. A plot is also a narrative of events, the emphasis falling on causality. 'The king died and then the queen died' is a story. 'The king died and then the queen died of grief' is a plot.[5]

For Forster, what distinguishes a plot from a story is the notion of causality: the sense that there is a causal relationship between the events in the narrative. However, many feel that this is a false distinction because when narratives convey more than one event in succession the reader will automatically assume a relationship between them, regardless of whether this has been made explicit. Shlomith Rimmon-Kenan in her book *Narrative Fiction: Contemporary Poetics*, for instance, argues that 'temporal succession is sufficient as a minimal requirement for a group of events to form a story'[6]. In Forster's

---

[5] Forster, E.M., *Aspects of the Novel* (London: Penguin Classics, 2005; originally published, 1927) p.87. All future references will be made to this edition.

[6] Rimmon-Kenan, Shlomith, *Narrative Fiction: Contemporary Poetics* (London: Methuen, 1983) p.18. All future references will be made to this edition.

example, 'The king died and then the queen died', the events are connected by the phrase 'and then'; it implies causality and so the story automatically becomes a plot in Forster's terms. For this reason many critics use the terms plot and story synonymously, and that will be the case in this book.

The Organisation of a Story

Angela Carter's novel *Wise Children* (1991) could usefully be employed to illustrate some aspects of story organisation. This novel takes the form of a first-person memoir narrated by an old lady called Dora Chance – she and her twin sister, Nora, are members of a theatrical family, and Dora's memoir presents a history of that family. The narrative – i.e. the telling of the story – begins and ends on the same day. It begins the morning of Dora and Nora's seventy-fifth birthday, and ends the same evening with a party. However, the *story* involves more than this. The story includes a sequence of events that goes right back to before Dora was born: it involves the entire history of her family, Dora's parents' history, and her grandparents' history. Carter doesn't begin her narrative with the history of the family; rather, she ignores story chronology and begins with a moment of crisis: the arrival of Dora's half-brother Tristram on her doorstep bringing news of the disappearance of his partner Tiffany. Only after stimulating our interest with this dramatic opening does the narrator begin to deliver details of the family's history that will provide the context for the novel. Thus the dramatic opening is followed by a long flashback that begins with the words: 'let us pause awhile in the unfolding story of Tristram and Tiffany ... '[7] This introduces a section where Dora's narrative goes back in time to relate the birth of her father, Melchoir, and her uncle Peregrine. Then the narrative returns again to Dora's present with more scenes of her and Tristram at home on her birthday, before going back in time again to relate more about the history of the family. Narratologists often use the terms analepsis and prolepsis for flashback and flash forward respectively. Both analepsis and prolepsis are sustained throughout *Wise Children*, although the novel spends more time in the past than it does in the present because this is where the primary story lies: with the history of Dora and Nora's family. The flashbacks themselves are not narrated in a linear way either: within the flashbacks we get more movement backwards and forwards in time. Most fictional narratives do this, of course, because stories need to be shaped in order to maximise their potential to engage readers. Like most novels, *Wise Children* dramatises some events and summarises others. The terms often used to describe drama and summary are mimesis and diegesis. In mimesis events are shown as they happen, while in diegesis they are summed-up by the narrator. If Dora dramatised the entire story of *Wise Children*, it would result in the longest book in the world, and the most boring. When events are dramatised, narrative time slows down and events are presented as they take place in real time. When events are

---

[7] Angela Carter, *Wise Children* (London: Chatto and Windus) p.11. All subsequent references will be to this edition.

summarised, the story speeds up. All storytellers have to decide which events to include in the story, and in what degree of detail. Events deemed to be particularly significant, for instance, might be the ones to dwell on in the form of a real-time scene; conversely, events can be summarised when such focus is not necessary. Consider the following scene from *Wise Children* when Tristram calls and asks Dora if she has seen his partner Tiffany:

> He hung on to me, panting for breath.
> 'Tiffany...' (pant, heave, pant) '... is Tiffany here?'
> 'Do pull yourself together Tristram, you've made a big wet patch on my silk,' I said sharply.
> 'Didn't you catch last night's programme?'
> 'You wouldn't catch me dead watching your poxy programme'(p.9).

This is an example of mimesis: the conversation between Dora and Tristram is a significant moment; the narrator slows things down in order to introduce an element of drama and narrative tension relating to Tristram's missing partner. The narrator could have had said, 'Tristram arrived and told us that Tiffany was missing', but this would constitute a diegetic summary of events which would not focus the reader's attention in quite the same way; as the disappearance introduces an element of suspense, it is important to foreground it. Compare this with the following:

> Here we sit, in our negligées, in the breakfast room in the leather armchairs by the Readicole electric fire. Sometimes we sit there all day, drink tea, chew the fat. Wheelchair plays solitaire, does the tapestry. The cats come and go.

> At six we switch to gin (p.8).

From the second sentence on, Dora sums-up the family's routine at their home in Bard Street, conveying their lifestyle over the years in a few short sentences. Narrating it mimetically would mean showing every day, exactly how it happened, in real time, which would obviously be impossible. Sometimes the terms mimesis and diegesis are equated with showing and telling: mimesis gives the impression of direct presentation, ostensibly unmediated by a narrator, while the narrator's 'telling' presence is more obvious in diegetic passages.

A narrative can vary the duration of events by other means too. Some critics use the terms slowdown, pause, and ellipsis to discuss how narrators create emphasis in a story, or make the shortcuts required to move a story along. Slowdowns and pauses occur when narrators include a significant amount of description or reflection. During a slowdown the narrator dwells on a scene to such an extent that narrative-time exceeds story-time. A pause takes this even further, and occurs when a narrator stays with a scene to elaborate extensively on it. At such points the story can seem to grind to a halt. Ellipses, meanwhile, refer to elements which are not actually narrated, but which are implied in the story. The narration of any tale requires ellipses, as the narrator of Laurence Sterne's novel *Tristram Shandy* (1767) observes. In the following quote the narrator – who has written several volumes of narrative – reflects on the progress of his autobiographical story:

> I am this month one whole year older than I was this time twelve-month; and having got, as you perceive,

> almost into the middle of my third volume – and no farther than to my first day's life – 'tis demonstrative that I have three hundred and sixty-four days more life to write just now, than when I first set out; so that instead of advancing, as a common writer, in my work with what I have been doing at it – on the contrary, I am just thrown so many volumes back – [8]

The narrator has been trying to write about his life but laments the fact that, while he has written much in terms of narrative, he has progressed little in terms of story; indeed, because he is a year older than when he began, he now has a longer story to tell than when he started! In other words, ellipsis and diegesis are necessary precisely because the whole story can never be told.

The Deep Structure of Stories

Some people argue that, at the deepest level, all stories are underpinned by a limited number of structures, and in this sense there are a finite number of stories. In *The Raw and the Cooked* (1964), for instance, the anthropologist Claude Lévi-Strauss studied the composition of myths and argued that they share a common structure, combining oppositional elements in similar ways. He felt that at their most basic level all myths move from a state of conflict to a state of resolution; all contain elements that oppose one another at the outset,

---

[8] Laurence Sterne, *The Life and Opinions of Tristram Shandy*, in *The Works of Laurence Stern in One Volume* (Philadelphia: Lippincott, Granbo and Co, 1854. First published in one volume, 1767) p.125.

together with elements that work to enable the apparent resolution of that opposition. Lévi-Strauss took what is known as a structuralist approach, a form of analysis that strives to identify the primary laws governing the combination of a story's component parts into meaning. It is a method that tends to focus on the form of a story rather than the content; it breaks a story down into units of signification and examines how these generate meaning in relation to one another. For example, a structuralist reading of the Dan Rhodes story 'Laughing' might identify the fundamental units of signification as life and death, in the sense that the hero's girlfriends are either alive or dead. This opposition exists alongside another opposition represented by the presence and absence of laughter. In this story life and laughter cannot exist simultaneously, just as life and death can't. The story provides a kind of resolution to the problem in the form of the final girlfriend who doesn't find the hero funny. Death is avoided, but at the price of laughter. Using this interpretation, the story would seem to suggest that life is dependent on a middle way, on compromise. Notice that with this approach the specific content of the story is not particularly important: laughter could be replaced by a fondness for jam tarts, and resolution could come in the form of a girlfriend who doesn't have a sweet tooth; either way, the fundamental meaning would be the same. Also, the narrative arrangement of the story is immaterial: both of the versions of the Rhodes story cited above would signify in the same way.

Structuralism has affinities with what is known as formalism, which also largely ignores the content of the story, focusing exclusively on form. The Russian scholar Vladímir Propp was an exponent of this approach, and in his book *The Morphology of the Folktale* (1928) he attempts to isolate the structural elements common to Russian folk tales. His method is different to Lévi-Strauss's in that, rather than seeking patterns or symbolic oppositions in stories, he is interested in the linear unfolding of events in a story, and how their component parts are organised chronologically. Propp identified a limited number of 'functions' – thirty-one in total – that recur in all Russian folk tales. For instance, the tales often involve a hero leaving home (function one in Propp's scheme), or a hero being told not to do something (function two), a hero violating that command (function three), a villain deceiving a hero (function six), a villain being defeated (function eighteen), a hero being finally recognised as a hero (function twenty-seven), and so on. According to Propp, whenever specific functions appear in a tale they always follow the same order. Propp's analysis of folk tales is convincing as far as it goes, and significant in demonstrating that certain stories have repeatable structures, but it is limited in that he does not say what implications these observations might have. What, for instance, might the occurrence and defeat of 'false heroes' tell us about the cultural context in which these tales were produced; or, more generally, about the human condition? To be fair, this wasn't Propp's intention, and it doesn't stop others using his structures to explore such questions.

A contemporary writer who examines deep structures and who *is* interested in interpreting their meaning is Christopher

Booker. Booker's *The Seven Basic Plots: Why We Tell Stories* (2004) has been dismissed by some commentators, but is widely discussed and certainly merits attention. As the title suggests, Booker identifies seven recurring plots or story structures:

- *Overcoming the Monster* These are stories in which the hero is in conflict with a dark force which threatens him as an individual, or humanity in general. This is the structure of the earliest recorded story, *The Epic of Gilgamesh* (2000 BC) and can be found in numerous contemporary tales, including James Bond stories.
- *Rags to Riches* These include simple fairy-tales like 'Cinderella' and 'The Ugly Duckling', as well as complex novels such as Charlotte Brontë's *Jane Eyre* (1847). In these stories initially unremarkable characters are revealed as heroic, or in some way special.
- *The Quest* In these stories the hero is forced to overcome hazards in order to reach a goal, and they include such narratives as Homer's *The Odyssey* (700 BC), or recent novels such as Charles Frazier's *Cold Mountain* (1997).
- *Voyage and Return* Here the hero moves from an environment of comfort into one of danger; good examples include stories such as Lewis Carroll's *Alice's Adventures in Wonderland* (1865) and H.G. Wells's *The Time Machine* (1895).
- *Comedy* Comic stories tend to involve the resolution of more complex problems; often this includes a confusion which impedes a relationship, but which is eventually overcome to allow an ending in marriage. Examples of classic comedies include

Shakespeare's *Twelfth Night* (1623) and Jane Austen's *Pride and Prejudice* (1813).
- *Tragedy* Here the hero suffers a fatal flaw that leads to his demise, a plot that underpins stories like Shakespeare's *King Lear* (1608) and Oscar Wilde's *The Picture of Dorian Grey* (1890).
- *Rebirth* In stories of rebirth the hero tends to be under the power of a dark force, experiencing a kind of living death; heroes are freed at the end, at which point they are metaphorically born again. Charles Dickens's *A Christmas Carol* (1843) might be seen as an example, as might tales such as 'The Frog King' or 'Little Briar Rose'.

Like Propp, Booker takes each plot-type and breaks it down into its constituent functions. For instance, the structure of 'overcoming the monster' stories splits into five parts, beginning with the 'anticipation' stage where the monster and the hero are introduced: here the hero gets the 'call' as he is made aware of his mission. The second stage is the 'dream stage' where the hero prepares for battle; at this point readers feel detached from the imminent threat, 'our feelings are still of a comfortable remoteness from and an immunity to danger.' The third stage is the 'frustration stage' where it looks as if the hero's task will never be realised. This is followed by the 'nightmare stage' when it appears the hero might be defeated by the monster. The fifth and final part is the 'thrilling escape from death and the death of monster'[9].

As an example, consider Ian McEwan's *Enduring Love*

---

[9] Christopher Booker, *The Seven Basic Plots: Why We Tell Stories* (London: Continuum, 2004) p.48. All further references will be to this edition.

(1997) – Booker does not mention it, but it clearly has an 'overcoming the monster' structure. It begins with the hero, Joe, and his partner Clarissa enjoying a picnic; this idyllic scene is disturbed when a hot-air balloon flies out of control in a nearby field. There is a child trapped on board, and when Joe joins a number of other people who attempt to assist, he witnesses the tragic death of one of the other helpers. This is the anticipation stage where Joe is introduced to the 'monster', a man called Jed Parry who had also joined the helpers, and who shows a peculiar interest in Joe. The hero gets a literal 'call' from Parry when he arrives home at the end of the day: bizarrely, Parry phones to tell Joe that he loves him. Joe seems instinctively aware of the threat that Parry poses, and the fact that he is an obsessive and destructive force – a monster. Joe responds to this in the 'dream stage' where he prepares himself for the battle that he anticipates. At first this involves arming himself emotionally by confiding in Clarissa about Parry's unhealthy obsession with him, and contacting the police. Clarissa feels that he is exaggerating, as do the police; readers are also unsure about the extent of the threat, we are made to feel remote from it and immune to it. The 'frustration' stage sees Parry becoming an increasing menace, however, and Joe can seemingly do nothing about it. In desperation, Joe purchases a gun in order to protect himself, but immediately after the purchase discovers that Parry has broken into his flat and is holding Clarissa hostage. This could be considered the 'nightmare' stage, where it seems as though the monster has the upper hand. The 'thrilling escape' follows as Joe manages to shoot Parry and free Clarissa. The monster, Parry, is only wounded but the novel closes with him confined to a mental institution, and Clarissa and Joe – after being estranged during the frustration and nightmare stages – are reconciled. In this sense the novel has a conventional happy ending, but qualified to some extent as the monster is not fully banished.

According to Booker, all plots, apart from tragedy, are meant to conclude happily, but stories underwent a shift during the era of Romanticism (1800-1840), a period he associates with a split between the Self and the Ego. Since then, though authors have continued to use the same basic structures in their stories, they often fail to be fully realised or resolved. Inspired by the theories of the psychoanalyst Carl Jung, Booker suggests that this failure is indicative of the dominance of the Ego in the modern world, and a lack of psychological integration. Indeed, I mentioned *Enduring Love* in particular because this seems like a perfect example of a story in which the basic 'monster' plot remains unresolved: as with many contemporary stories the threat of darkness is not completely eradicated. At the end, Parry is confined, but he lives on, and it is made clear that his pathological obsession with Joe is undiminished. However, Booker feels that 'good' stories are still in evidence in the modern world, and he cites Tolkien's *The Lord of the Rings* (1954) as an example. This actually incorporates all of the seven basic plots in its various storylines, and for Booker the power of Tolkien's plot is further 'reinforced' by Peter Jackson's film version. Unlike many modern stories, darkness is defeated by light in a completely satisfying way at the end, principally because its hero Frodo Baggins finally manages to free himself from 'the beguiling power of the ego,' and devote himself to the cause of destroying the ring (p.694). This is not the best example Booker could give, however, as he seems to miss the fact that Frodo actually fails in his mission both in the novel and the film. He is overcome with desire to keep the ring for himself, and it is ultimately destroyed by accident when Gollum steals it from Frodo and falls into the Cracks of Doom: the point seems to be that only divine intervention can overcome such profound evil.

Booker believes that all stories are essentially didactic, teaching the same essential message that we should resist being 'ego-centred'. He argues that the terms hero and heroine must be etymologically related to the term heir – 'he or she who is born to inherit; who is worthy to succeed; who must grow up as fit to take on the torch of life from those who went before' (p.702). Basically the implication is that when someone becomes a true hero in the fullest sense – when the plot structure is satisfactorily resolved – this offers an example of how to live in the world. Regardless of how much credence we give to give Booker's ideas, his work is a good example of how a reflection on deep structure might offer insights into the function of storytelling in our lives.

Structure for Creative Writers

The kind of structures mentioned here are potentially valuable for creative writers. Certainly some writers find it beneficial to construct an overarching plot-plan before they begin to create narratives. Asking questions about the kind of story you are writing (e.g. quest, rags to riches, voyage and return) can help determine narrative form, and broadly establish a sense of how characters should be developed and what their trajectory should be. This is particularly useful with longer narratives such as novels. Novelists without a plan risk losing their way, and their focus: using a plot-plan or framework can help writers orientate material and determine what is relevant and what is not. Plot-plans are also useful for pacing narratives, and determining where and when key scenes should be introduced. So, for instance, Nigel Watts in his book *Writing a Novel* (2003) suggests the following 'eight point arc' as a basic structure for novel writers:

> • *Stasis* This is what Watts refers to as the 'base reality of the tale', which could be seen as the status quo that precedes the conflict.[10]
>
> • *Trigger* Watts calls this 'an event beyond the control of the [protagonist] which turns the day from average to exceptional'(p.28). In other words, something happens to upset the status quo and create conflict.
>
> • *The Quest* The trigger creates 'a quest for the protagonist. In the case of an unpleasant trigger the quest is often to return to the original stasis; in that of a pleasant trigger the quest is often to maintain or increase the pleasure.' (p.29).Essentially the quest is to resolve the conflict created by the trigger.
>
> • *Surprise* Watts says that 'Characters need to experience obstacles [and] unexpected things must happen' (p.29).

---

[10] Nigel Watts, *Writing a Novel* (London: Hodder and Stoughton, 2003) p.28. All future references will be made to this edition.

The anticipation of the unexpected is, of course, a way of creating narrative tension.

- *Critical Choice* The characters need to be seen to be making decisions. It is hard to create stories around characters who are free from problems. One of the ways of engaging readers in a story is to make them care about how characters deal with their problems. Also, Watts suggests that 'unless the character is accountable in some sense for his or her actions we have accident and coincidence and chaos', which will be unlikely to command the sustained attention of a modern reader (p.30).
- *Climax* For Watts, critical choices 'come to a head in the form of a climax [...] A surprise could be a burglar breaking into a house; the critical choice of the householder is self-defence, the climax is the burglar being hit over the head' (pp.30-31).
- *Reversal* A reversal is 'the consequence of previous events.' This is what gives the climax meaning for Watts; without an adequate reversal a reader can be left with the feeling that the climax exists purely for the sake of spectacle. The reversal alters the situation of the characters in a meaningful way and should develop out of the climax as if it is 'inevitable and probable' (pp.31-32).
- *Resolution* This equates to the re-establishment of stasis.

Many others have offered similar structures as aids to fiction writers, but Watts's arc seems particularly workable. Certainly many novel-length stories adhere to this basic structure. To again take the example of McEwan's *Enduring Love*, the initial picnic scenes in the opening chapter of this novel might constitute the base reality or stasis stage of the story, while the accident that introduces Parry – Joe's stalker – becomes the trigger which disrupts the hero's life. As the introduction of Parry is an unpleasant trigger, the hero's quest from thereon is to return to the comfortable status quo of the stasis. Joe experiences several surprises, mainly taking the form of Parry's various encroachments on his life; he must respond to these accordingly, and his responses constitute his choices, the fifth point on the arc. This is what sustains our engagement with the novel, the most basic and crucial aspect of the storyteller's art: the anticipation of what a character is going to do next. The critical choice that precipitates the climax of McEwan's novel is Joe's purchase of a gun: here the hero opts to take the law into his own hands following the police's reluctance to take his fears about Parry seriously. This climax is given meaning by his decision to use the gun, which prompts the reversal where Joe shoots his nemesis; following this reversal Joe and Clarissa are able to resume their relationship, allowing the reestablishment of the status quo, and the resolution of the story.

Of course, there are much simpler ways to conceive of plot – beginning, middle and end, for one; or, even more succinctly, conflict and response. Though not all writers are comfortable with elaborate plot-plans, all must give some thought as to where conflict resides, how characters are going to respond to that conflict, and how tension is to be sustained. All viable stories must create conflict, and raise questions about how characters are going to deal with it. We read to discover what's going to happen next, and if this basic question isn't at the heart of a narrative then there is no story.

Who Tells the Story?

Generally speaking there are two main narrative strategies that storytellers tend to use: first person (I wrote a story) and third person (s/he wrote a story). Some stories do employ the second person (you wrote a story) but these are less common. The latter can be very effective, however, as in a novel such as Iain Banks's *Complicity* (1993), which juxtaposes first- and second-person narration. The first-person sections are told from the point of view of a journalist, Cameron, while the second-person sections offer the perspective of an unnamed serial killer. The effect is quite unsettling as it forces the reader into the situation of the killer: the constant reiteration of the pronoun 'you' establishes identification with the anonymous narrator, to some extent obliging readers to fill the identity gap against their will. Another alternative to conventional first- and third-person narration is the first-person plural (we wrote a story). This is very rare, but one good example is Joshua Ferris's *Then We Came To The End* (2007) – a novel set in a failing American advertising company. The story is told via the narrative 'we', representing the whole workforce as a single voice. The book implies that the individual has been subsumed by the collective, and in this sense is suggestive of how one can lose identity and individuality in the corporate world. As the advertising company gradually makes more and more of its staff redundant, the narrative 'we' becomes increasingly diminished, reflecting the slow death of the firm. In effect, the gradual expiration of the collective storyteller parallels the demise of the story's subject.

Despite some interesting exceptions, first- and third-person narratives dominate in fiction, and so the focus in this section will be on these. Before going on to address some examples, however, it is worth introducing some terminology.

Narrative Levels

Narratologists often refer to a typology of narrators in order to distinguish between types of storyteller, and their relationship to the story. Some of the terms used to describe levels of narration are listed below.

> •*Extradiegetic* This narrator is outside the story; they do not inhabit the story-world created by their narrative – they narrate, as it were, from a higher point.
>
> •*Intradiegetic* This is a second-level narrator, narrating within the story.
>
> •*Hypodiegetic* This narrator tells a story within an intradiegetic narrative, in other words adding yet another level of narration.

These terms refer to how the narrator relates to the world of the story (sometimes called the diegetic level: the level of the characters' world). For example, because the narrators of such novels as Henry Fielding's *Tom Jones* (1749) or George Eliot's *Middlemarch* (1874) lie outside the story-world they are deemed extradiegetic. However, if the first narrative contains another narrator, that narrator is deemed to be intradiegetic; these most often take the form of character-narrators. An often-cited example of this is Charlie Marlow in Joseph Conrad's *Heart of Darkness* (1899). In this novel an anonymous extradiegetic narrator describes a group of people aboard a boat anchored on the River Thames. They include a character called Charlie Marlow who begins to tell them a tale about his journey up-river in Africa searching for the mysterious man named Kurtz. Marlow is an intradiegetic narrator because he exists within the world of the story – at the diegetic level – as a character. If another storyteller is introduced at this level (i.e. framed by an intradiegetic narrator), they are called hypodiegetic: an example of which can be found in Henry James's famous novella, *The Turn of the Screw* (1898). Here again there is an anonymous extradiegetic narrator (referred to as 'I'), an intradiegetic narrator called Douglas, and another narrator, narrating within Douglas's narrative: the children's governess, who is a hypodiegetic narrator.

There are also a number of terms that narratologists use to denote the degree of participation of narrators in the stories they tell.

- *Heterodiegetic* This is a narrator who is not present as a character in the story at all.
- *Homodiegetic* This is a character-narrator who is present in the story to some degree.
- *Autodiegetic* This term is used when the homodiegetic narrator is also the protagonist of the story: i.e. a hero-narrator.

The narrator of a novel like Henry Fielding's *Tom Jones* is not only extradiegetic, but also heterodiegetic, because he is outside the story, and never features in it to any degree. An example that Shlomith Rimmon-Kenan offers of an intradiegetic-heterodiegetic narrator is the Miller in Chaucer's *The Canterbury Tales*: he exists at the level of a story created by a higher narrator, and within that story he relates another story that he himself does not participate in; however, Chaucer's Pardoner, who occupies the same narrative level as the Miller but who *does* feature in the story he tells, constitutes an intradiegetic-homodiegetic narrator. Pip, the narrator-hero of Charles Dickens's *Great Expectations* (1861), is called an extradiegetic-homodiegetic narrator by Rimmon-Kenan because he narrates the story of his own youth from his perspective as an adult: in other words as an adult he is outside the story (extradiegetic), but because it's about his youth he is obviously also part of it (homodiegetic); it is also legitimate to refer to Pip as an autodiegetic narrator because of his status as narrator-protagonist.

Focalisation

When studying narratives, it is useful to make a distinction between narration and focalisation. The latter is occasionally described as narrative point of view, perspective or viewpoint, and it is meant to refer to the perceiving consciousness in a story. The focaliser is *not* necessarily the same as narrator, of course, because there can be a distinction between who tells, and who perceives the story. Consider the opening of William Faulkner's short story, 'Barn Burning':

> The store in which the Justice of the Peace's court was sitting smelled of cheese. The boy, crouched on his nail keg at the back of the crowded room, knew he smelled cheese, and more: from where he sat he could see the ranked shelves close-packed with the solid, squat, dynamic shapes of tin cans whose labels his stomach read, not from the lettering which meant nothing to his mind but from the scarlet devils and the silver curve of fish – this, the cheese which he knew he smelled and the hermetic meat which his intestines believed he smelled coming in intermittent gusts momentary and brief between the other constant one, the smell and sense just a little of fear because mostly of despair and grief, the old fierce pull of blood.[11]

This is a third-person, extradiegetic-heterodiegetic narrator (i.e. outside the story and playing no part in it), but there is a clear internal perspective that belongs to the boy; we see and smell the room from his point of view: he can see 'the ranked shelves' and he can smell the cheese. So the boy is the focaliser here, even though the voice is that of the narrator. The latter's language is too mature and sophisticated to belong to the boy: he would not use words like 'hermetic' and 'intermittent'. While some third-person stories limit their focalisation to one perspective, of course, others present their stories from a variety of perspectives and switch between them.

---

[11] William Faulkner, 'Barn Burning'. In Donald McQuade (ed.), *The Harper American Literature Volume Two* (New York: Harper Collins, 1993) pp.1137-1149

First-Person Narrators

There can also be a distinction between narration and focalisation in first-person narratives. The example Rimmon-Kenan gives is Pip, the narrator of *Great Expectations*. As mentioned earlier, though this novel is narrated by the adult Pip, much of the story concerns the experiences of a younger Pip. In the scenes where Pip is a child, events are seen from his perspective: he is the focaliser; but the narrator is the adult Pip who, again, often reveals himself through his use of a vocabulary that is too sophisticated for a child. This is frequently the case in retrospective first-person narratives, and is sometimes referred to as double focalisation: the narrative has a twin perspective, that of a younger self who experienced events, and that of an older, narrating self whose perspective is broader and more informed. Narrators can view events from outside or inside a story, then, and this is referred to as external and internal focalisation respectively. An external focaliser can offer a bird's eye view of events, and see everything from outside; internal focalisation provides a perspective from inside the story, employing a character as the perceiving consciousness. Obviously focalisation is central to how we experience the events of the story, and an example of how it can function that is worth looking at in some detail is F. Scott Fitzgerald's novel *The Great Gatsby* (1925).

The Great Gatsby is narrated from the point of view of a character called Nick Carraway, and the story details his experiences as a younger man in New York, specifically his relationship with one man, Jay Gatsby. Carraway is both an external and an internal focaliser: he makes reference to both the narrative present, and the fact that he has a broad, complete view of everything in his story. For instance, in the very first chapter he tells us about returning home after his time in the East, and the fact that 'Gatsby turned out alright in the end', which clearly demonstrates external focalisation and even hints at how the story ends and how we might interpret it.[12] However, Nick is mostly an internal focaliser *within* the story itself, and on these occasions he has a limited knowledge of the world in which his younger self moves. Thus, he presents himself as someone who doesn't know who Gatsby is or where he came from or how he made his fortune (things that he clearly *does* know because he's telling the tale retrospectively). There are obvious reasons why Fitzgerald presents the majority of the novel in this way. Jay Gatsby's status as a mysterious character at the beginning of the novel, for instance, drives the plot to a large extent, and so this mystery needs to be preserved. Writing is partly about creating such questions and then drip-feeding the answers to the reader; withholding the older and wiser Nick Carraway's information is crucial because to tell it would spoil the story. This, then, is one reason why Fitzgerald moves from broad external focalisation to limited internal focalisation. Another involves the way in which the novel sets up a moral distinction between the young Carraway and the older Carraway. Nick narrates the story from a time two years after the events have concluded; this older Nick is no longer in New York as he

---

[12] F. Scott Fitzgerald, *The Great Gatsby* (Middlesex: Penguin, 1986; first published 1926) p.167. All future references will be made to this edition.

tells his story – he has moved back West. In effect, he is telling us what happened to him when he was in the big city now that he is safely home. The idea of him being back in the West is important because geography is symbolic in the novel. In the moral scheme of *The Great Gatsby* the East is associated with the pursuit of wealth and a lack of real values. Conversely the West is a place which still manages to preserve genuine, traditional moral values. At the end of the story Carraway returns West because he sees it as a region where society and social conduct are founded on something more meaningful than the pursuit of money. In one sense, Fitzgerald's novel is a like a 'voyage and return' story in which the hero has travelled East only to return home a wiser man. Nick – the younger, internal focaliser – is naïve compared to the mature, external Nick who now has a more sophisticated understanding of moral issues. At the outset, Nick tells us that he never judges people because his father warned him not to: 'just remember that all the people in this world haven't had the advantages that you've had' (p.7). Early in his story the younger Nick largely succeeds in following this advice, yet by the end he no longer refrains from condemning those who behave immorally, as his mature assessment of Tom and Daisy makes clear:

> They were careless people, Tom and Daisy – they smashed up things and creatures and then retreated back into their money or their vast carelessness, or whatever it was that kept them together, and let other people clean up the mess they had made (p.170).

So Nick learns something throughout the course of the book – he learns that it's not always possible to sit on the fence: when you think something is wrong you have to say so. The juxtaposition of the younger, naïve Nick's internal focalisation with the older Nick's more mature and informed perspective works to underscore this point.

Unreliable Narrators

In a manner of speaking, all first-person narrators are potentially unreliable. Given that they represent a single viewpoint, their perspective is, by implication, subjective. In most novels this isn't important, and it doesn't make much difference whether we consider the narrator fallible or not. However, some novels make an issue of the narrator's untrustworthiness. A text might include various clues that lead us to speculate about whether we are meant to question a narrator's reliability: as will be seen, this might include the narrator's age or state of mind, or a possible penchant for duplicity evidenced by discrepancies between the narrator's assertions and those of other characters.

Idiosyncratic Narrators

Some narrators can be unreliable not because they lie, but because they have an unconventional view of the world: their perspective may be limited in some way, or eccentric. One example is Christopher, the autodiegetic narrator of Mark Haddon's *The Curious Incident of the Dog in the Night-Time* (2003). The fact that Christopher has Asperger's syndrome means that he sees the world in a very literal and unsubtle way. He doesn't understand metaphors, for instance, so when his mother calls him 'the apple of her eye' this confuses him because he is not *literally* an apple. He thinks that metaphor is a form of lying. He is also limited socially because, among other things, he cannot understand facial expressions. So, when talking about his father, he says, 'He looked at me for a long time and sucked air in through his nose'[13] the reader knows that this is because his father is furious with him, but Christopher doesn't understand. Sometimes this creates humour, but often it is sad, and sometimes terrifying – when Christopher tells us he's about to do something that we know isn't in his best interests, or which might even put his life in danger, the experience is rather like being in a nightmare (such as when he saves his pet rat, who has scurried onto the tracks of the London Underground). Importantly, he is not an unreliable narrator in the sense that he does not tell the truth: he always tells the truth, it is just his version of reality is profoundly idiosyncratic. Because the focalisation is always internal – i.e. confined to Christopher's limited perspective – we are never given a broader view of his experiences; we are forced to see things as he sees them. It might be said that his view of the world can teach us something important; it invites us to reflect on what

---

[13] Mark Haddon, *The Curious Incident of the Dog in the Night-Time* (London: Vintage, 2012; first published 2003) p.27

a strange place our apparently normal world seems when it is described in literal terms and, given the behaviour of the adults in Christopher's life, it also makes us speculate about where dysfunction ends and so-called normality begins.

Naïve Narrators

As suggested, when determining whether we are meant to question the narrator's reliability, we need to look for signs. One sign might be the age of the protagonist: an autodiegetic child narrator – where the narrator and the focaliser are one and the same – would of necessity offer a limited perspective on the world. Another indicator might have to do with references to the narrator's state of mind. A novel whose narrator raises questions both of maturity and mental stability is J.D. Salinger's *The Catcher in the Rye* (1951). The protagonist-narrator's name is Holden Caulfield; he is a sixteen-year-old boy suffering a mental breakdown, and we quickly learn that his understanding of his world – and his understanding of himself – is a little limited. The novel opens in the following way:

> If you really want to hear about it, the first thing you'll probably want to know is where I was born, and what my lousy childhood was like, and how my parents were occupied and all before they had me, and all that David Copperfield kind of crap, but I don't feel like going into it, if you want to know the truth. In the first place, that stuff bores me, and in the second place, my parents would have about two

> haemorrhages apiece if I told anything pretty personal about them. They're quite touchy about anything like that, especially my father. They're *nice* and all – I'm not saying that – but they're also touchy as hell. Besides, I'm not going to tell you my whole goddam autobiography or anything. I'll just tell you about this madman stuff that happened to me around last Christmas just before I got pretty run-down and had to come out here and take it easy. I mean that's all I told D.B. about, and he's my *brother* and all. He's in Hollywood. That isn't too far from this crumby place, and he comes over and visits me practically every week end. He's going to drive me home when I go home next month maybe.[14]

The nature of the language gives us some clues to the age and attitude of the narrator – it is replete with exaggeration, and verbal ticks ('an all') that are reminiscent of a garrulous adolescent. At this point in the book – before he actually starts to tell us his story – we are still in the narrative present, and he makes several remarks that raise questions about his state of mind. He has experienced some 'madman stuff' that he is about to convey to us, but while it's suggested that this is in the past, it's by no means clear that he has *fully* recovered. He mentions that he will be going home next month, but this is qualified by the word 'maybe'; undoubtedly, it is significant that he has yet to be released. As with Nick Carraway, there is a distinction between internal and external focalisers (the younger and the slightly older Holden

---

[14] J.D. Salinger, *The Catcher in the Rye* (London: Penguin, 1994; first published, 1951) p.1

respectively), but we can't be *absolutely* sure about the state of mind of either.

Throughout the course of the novel, Holden continually accuses adults of being phony: everywhere he looks in life people appear duplicitous, and he is immensely disillusioned by this. Ostensibly the adult world condemns lies, but adults habitually contravene their professed standards. His parents lie, his teachers lie, Hollywood films lie – hypocrisy is everywhere. However, as the story progresses we see Holden lying too: he exaggerates, he adopts false identities, and he casually deceives people whenever he feels like it. This, in itself, constitutes evidence of his potential unreliability; it also demonstrates that he can't live up to the standards that he sets for others: he is just as big a hypocrite as the people he censures. Holden's ambition is to be a 'catcher in the rye', which to him means protecting children's innocence and saving them from the 'fall' into the corrupt world of adulthood; however, his own inability to adhere to the standards he sets suggests that his expectations are too high, that this idealism isn't a viable way of living in the world. His standards are at odds with human nature, including his own. During the novel, there are some indications that the mature Holden might be beginning to grasp this – he makes some comments to this effect, and it is hinted that he may be ready to return to society, free of his pathological cynicism – but again this is not certain. Importantly, though there are signs that Holden is on the road to recovery, we cannot be sure, and this uncertainty continues to the close, creating an ambiguous end to the story. Arguably this ambiguity makes for a better novel: on the one hand, having Holden continue in his psychosis would be an unsatisfactory, escapist ending to the story; on the other hand, having Holden cured and reconciled to society at the end wouldn't work either – it would undermine the hero's criticism of twentieth-century America and the corruption and hypocrisy associated with it. As it stands, the novel works a little like Mark Haddon's in that Holden's naïve perspective forces the reader to ponder the nature of hypocrisy and value in the modern world: the reader is meant to see at least *some* wisdom in Holden's naïvety.

A different kind of naïvety can be found in certain geriatric narrators. One example is Dora, the narrator of Carter's novel, *Wise Children*. Dora is seventy-five years old and she and her sister are the illegitimate daughters of a Shakespearian actor. Dora is writing her memoirs, a history of her family, and the narrative proceeds from this premise. Dora can be considered fallible in her representation of events for a variety of reasons: many took place when she was a child, some took place before she was born, and, of course, she is old. Indeed, Dora is always drawing the reader's attention to her unreliability: she says things like, 'it *was* sixty-odd years ago', and, 'I might think I did not live but dreamed that night'. *Wise Children* has been called a work of magic realism, and though the story is not overly fantastical, odd things do often occur – events that cannot be reconciled with the real world. In this sense it is helpful for Carter to have an unreliable narrator: when narrating something that is hard to square with realism, Dora can be vague about exactly what happened, putting distance between the reader and the novel's occasionally unrealistic events. For example, at one point we're told:

> Peregrine swept us into his arms. Then when our father denied us, Peregrine spread his arms as wide as wings and gathered up the orphan girls ... or perhaps he slipped us one in each pocket of his jacket ... And then, hup, he did a back-flip out of the window with us ... But I know I'm imagining the back-flip (p.72).

Dora admits to imagining the back-flip, but what about Peregrine putting her and her sister in his pockets? It may be that she is relating the essence of the experience, rather than the literal facts, but having a potentially unreliable narrator like Dora means we expect less from her in terms of precision: we can more readily forgive ambiguity, exaggeration, vagueness, and those elements that contribute to the narrative's patina of fantasy and strangeness.

Insane Narrators

Another interesting unreliable narrator is Patrick Bateman, the protagonist of Bret Easton Ellis's *American Psycho* (1991). Bateman claims to be a serial killer, and he is unreliable because we cannot be absolutely sure that this is the case. While in *Catcher* we are given an – albeit qualified – mature perspective on the narrator's strange ideas, we do not get this in *American Psycho*. As we are only presented with Bateman's view of the world – i.e. a potentially insane internal focalisation – it is difficult to know where reality ends and his possible insanity begins. The unreliability is created by a possible discrepancy between what Bateman says and thinks about himself, and what other people say about him (as reported to us by Bateman himself). So while Bateman claims to be a serial killer, his friends and colleagues' responses to him often suggest otherwise: his girlfriend Evelyn refers to him as 'the boy next door', for instance; and, after confessing to his supposed killings on his lawyer's answer phone, his lawyer refuses to believe him, calling him a 'goody-goody'[15]. Also, many of the victims of his alleged crimes are nameless vagrants and loners, and so there is no real evidence that he has committed them. Indeed, it is difficult to give credence to some of the killings he describes: they often seem almost comically over-the-top to the point where we have to question their authenticity. The fact that the novel is set in 1980s America gives this an extra dimension: the novel makes the point that modern America often appears so bizarre that it's difficult to be sure which bits of Patrick Bateman's experiences are credible representations of American life, and which bits are the ranting of a liar or madman. So here again the notion of unreliability is a key factor in how the book signifies.

---

[15] See Jennifer Phillips, 'Unreliable Narration in Bret Easton Ellis' *American Psycho*: Interaction Between Narrative Form and Thematic Content'. *Current Narratives, University of Wollongong* (undated) pp.60-69. http://currentnarratives.com/issues/pdfs/Phillips.pdf

First-Person Narrators of Other People's Stories

Homodiegetic narrators are not always central to the stories they tell, of course. *The Great Gatsby* is a bit like this – though it is partly Nick's story, the titular hero is Gatsby. Presenting Gatsby from the point of view of another character is an excellent strategy. We mentioned above that Gatsby is an enigmatic figure: he is a creature of myth and legend when Carraway first hears about him, and the truth is only gradually revealed to the reader. A sense of Gatsby's glamour and mystery is created partly by the fact that we only ever see him through Nick eyes – so there is always a distance between the reader and the character. If we were able to observe Gatsby too closely (say if we were given access to his consciousness) this effect would be ruined. It is much more effective to show Gatsby from the perspective of someone who is intrigued by him and, initially at least, a little in awe of him. So here the homodiegetic narrator acts as a useful filtering device which creates an essential space between a character and the reader. Another illustration of this might be Arthur Conan Doyle's Sherlock Holmes stories. Again, these are mainly told in the first person, but not for the most part by Holmes: all but four are narrated by his friend Dr Watson (only two are narrated by Holmes, while two are omniscient). One of the great things about these stories is the character of Sherlock Holmes himself – our sense of his genius and eccentricity. In some respects this is dependent on him remaining a remote character, not least because if we were given access to his mind he could never live up to our expectations. There is always something that must remain unknowable about Holmes, as otherwise his impact and appeal might be diminished. The fact that we mainly see him from Watson's perspective allows the necessary detachment to be maintained: Watson is the reader's eyes in the stories; like us, he is a mere mortal, there to be bewildered and impressed by the enigmatic genius.

First-Person Narrators and Emotional Engagement

Another reason why writers might choose a first-person character-narrator is to personalise the narration, as it can potentially establish a more intimate relationship with readers. Readers identify more readily with character-narrators than with anonymous voices. The impression is that they are speaking directly to us, confiding in us, and this has the potential to create a bond between narrator and reader. The more intimately we know a character the easier it is for us to empathise with them, and relate to their world and their reasons for doing things. One modern example is the narrator of Khaled Hosseini's *The Kite Runner* (2003). This is told by an Afghan man living in America called Amir, and the story is essentially about his life, and how his relationship with his friend, Hassan (who we later learn is his half-brother), affects it. Amir tells us about his early life and how, when he was young and living in Afghanistan, Amir behaved very badly toward Hassan: he did nothing to help him on an occasion when he was physically attacked, and he framed him as a thief, thereby disgracing Hassan and his family. Thanks to the autodiegetic strategy and the feeling of familiarity this promotes, we feel we have a connection with Amir and an emotional involvement in his behaviour, so-much-so that when he lets his friend down there is a sense in which he lets us down too. *The Kite Runner* develops into a story about Amir's attempt to atone for what he did to Hassan, and we are arguably more interested in this as readers because the intimate nature of the narration has given us a deeper understanding of what this means to Amir psychologically; it is more compelling and convincing because we have witnessed the extent of Amir's shame and his guilt, as it were, first hand. And, importantly, because we have this close and comprehensive insight into Amir, we are more able to sympathise with him too. If a stranger told a story about having done nothing to help a friend who was being assaulted, and then went on to frame them as a thief, it would be hard to sympathise. But, Amir does not feel like a stranger; we feel we know him; we are aware of various mitigating psychological factors (such as Amir's desperate need to impress his father) and, as a result, are more able to be tolerant of his transgression. In short, the use of a first-person narrator in *The Kite Runner* augments our emotional investment in the story.

Another important thing about first-person narrators is that readers don't expect them to be objective: because they are presented as human beings, they are allowed to be biased. This subjectivity – and the reader's acceptance of it – can be used to interesting effect when it comes to the presentation of other characters in stories. When Amir discusses his old friend Hassan in *The Kite Runner*, the image we get of him is hopelessly idealistic. Hassan seems like the perfect boy: loyal, friendly, morally upstanding, and completely flawless. He becomes a saint-like creature of a kind that would ordinarily be hard to believe in. If the description had come from an anonymous third-person narrator, rather than through a character-narrator, it would be difficult to accept; readers would find it hard to tolerate such an idealised, sentimental and essentially inauthentic representation of another human being. Readers allow it from a character-narrator because they allow for their partiality: they feel that it is just their opinion of this character. This is an important difference between first-person narrators and third-person narrators that will be addressed in more detail below.

First-Person Narration and Questions of Value

The reader's potential tolerance of a character-narrator's subjectivity can be important when it comes to the representation of controversial issues, and questions of value. Again, Fitzgerald's *The Great Gatsby* offers a useful example. As suggested, Gatsby is seen only from Nick Carraway's perspective, and Nick's moral evaluation of him is interesting. In the first few pages he tells us that Gatsby represents something for which he has 'unaffected scorn', on the one hand, while, on the other, he feels that 'there was something gorgeous about him', and that he 'turned out all right in the end' (p.8). Gatsby, of course, is a morally dubious character

– he is a crook who made his vast fortune from organised crime: the title of the book is ironic in the sense that Gatsby is not 'great'. In some respects, Gatsby is also a fool who invests everything in winning the love of a woman who is clearly not worth the effort. Gatsby moves in a world that is superficial and materialistic too, and in many ways he is emblematic of that world. By most criteria, then, Gatsby would be found wanting. However, Nick's assessment of Gatsby is a 'human' one, sensitive to potential moral complexity: Gatsby has redeeming qualities that Nick values; while his desire to win Daisy might be deluded, it reveals Gatsby's optimism, his integrity, and his capacity to love, and this influences Nick's assessment of his friend. Nick's subjectivity is interesting in other ways too. Though he ostensibly condemns the excesses of New York society, there is a sense in which Nick Carraway is captivated by its opulence. His lyrical and celebratory descriptions of it leave the reader with the impression that Nick is half in love with the things he is supposed to condemn. In other words, he is able to be seduced by the kind of things that Gatsby – and most of us – are drawn to, even against our will, and he is realistic enough to know that morality isn't always simple. It would be harder to provide this 'human' assessment of Gatsby and his world via an anonymous, extradiegetic narrator: as will be seen later, we expect objectivity from such a narrator; in *Gatsby* the perspective of a fallible character-narrator with an emotional investment in the story he tells is absolutely apposite.

Another example of a character-narrator's subjectivity influencing how we relate to a story can be found in Emily

Brontë's *Wuthering Heights* (1847). In part this is the story of a doomed relationship between two hot-headed characters, Catherine and Heathcliff. We get the story in the form a diary kept by a visitor to the area, Lockwood (an intradiegetic-homodiegetic narrator), and in this diary he tells of his encounter with a woman called Nelly Dean. Nelly tells him the story of Heathcliff and Catherine and he writes it up in his diary: so Nelly is a hypodiegetic-homodiegetic narrator, and Lockwood is the narratee (the one who is addressed by the narrative). In telling this story Nelly is quite critical of both Heathcliff and Catherine: Heathcliff is depicted as cruel, Catherine as spoilt and selfish. However, in the various conversations Nelly has with Lockwood, she herself is revealed as being rather judgemental in her attitudes, and not that good at reading people and relationships. She thinks, for instance, that Lockwood would make a good match for Catherine's daughter, when most people would feel that this isn't the case. Her narrative suggests that her thinking is very orthodox too, and that she does not really appreciate Catherine and Heathcliff's profound love for one another. One of the key scenes in *Wuthering Heights* is when Catherine says to Nelly that it would degrade her to marry Heathcliff. After she says this, Nelly sees that Heathcliff has overheard, but she doesn't say anything to Catherine. She doesn't tell her because she thinks it's better for Catherine to marry the rich Edgar Linton as opposed to the penniless Heathcliff. This act effectively destroys Catherine. Later, when Heathcliff disappears as a result of what he's heard, Nelly exonerates herself of blame and places the guilt for her own actions on

Catherine. So this tells us something important about Nelly – she is a character who doesn't take responsibility for her own actions. We know that we've been told the story by someone who makes mistakes, who is rather harsh and puritanical in her judgements, and who seems to be in denial about her own culpability in the tragic tale. Where the reader might have been inclined to view Catherine and Heathcliff negatively if their story had been told by an anonymous narrator, we're wary of doing that due to Nelly's unreliability. It adds another layer of complexity to the novel, and underscores one of the points the book makes about the dangers of seeing things in too simplistic a way. This is something that Heathcliff is guilty of – he thinks everything falls into black and white categories, that things are either right or wrong, good or bad; but life isn't that simple, and Emily Brontë's use of an unreliable narrator works to emphasise that point.

Third-Person Narrators

Third person narration usually indicates anonymous narrators who refer to the characters in the grammatical third person: s/he, they, it, etc. This is the most frequently used narrative strategy among storytellers as it allows for the greatest degree of flexibility given that narrators are not confined to a single perspective as they are in the first person.

Authorial Narrators

Authorial narration is a term occasionally used to refer to exclusively heterodiegetic narrators who don't feature in the story in any sense. They usually narrate in the third person, although sometimes – particularly in pre-twentieth-century novels – they may refer to themselves as the storyteller, interrupting and commenting on the story in the first person. One example is the narrator of Henry Fielding's *Tom Jones* (1749). Consider this narrative interruption to chapter two of Fielding's novel:

> Reader, I think proper, before we proceed any farther together, to acquaint thee that I intend to digress, through this whole history, as often as I see occasion, of which I am myself a better judge than any pitiful critic whatever.[16]

This narrator is not a character in the story, but he often steps into it to comment on the action, and to offer his opinion on the characters and their behaviour. Narrators who foreground their presence in this way are sometimes called overt narrators. Fielding's narrator, like most third-person narrators, also exhibits a degree of omniscience, and has a godlike, 'all-seeing' perspective on the events of the story. Such narrators limit their omniscience, of course, and like any narrator they select what to convey and when, using a mixture of external and internal focalisation to render their story. As we've seen, external focalisation occurs when the

---

[16] Henry Fielding, *Tom Jones* (Digireads: Digireads.com Publishing, 2009. First published, 1749) p.19. All future references will be to this edition.

point of view is with the narrator; internal focalisation occurs when it is with a character in the story; typically an authorial third-person narrator will move from one to another as appropriate. Sometimes authorial third-person narrators use numerous internal focalisers; sometimes they will be limited to one or two. In Jane Austen's *Pride and Prejudice* (1813), for instance, the narrator concentrates mainly on Elizabeth Bennett, and much is seen from her perspective; but the narrator is not limited to Elizabeth's point of view the way a first-person narrator would be: Austen's extradiegetic-heterodiegetic narrator is able to move beyond Elizabeth's perspective at will, conveying things that Elizabeth doesn't know, and talking generally about characters and events, as well as philosophising about the nature of life in a voice that is not linked to any character. So the famous opening line of the novel – 'It is a truth universally acknowledged, that a single man in possession of a good fortune must be in want of a wife' – does not employ Elizabeth's voice; it is the voice of the anonymous heterodiegetic narrator. Elizabeth has a much more realistic view of the world, and the more we are exposed to her views – views that undermine this so-called 'truth' – the more we begin to see that the opening statement is ironic.

The problem with many authorial narrators in early novels is that, unlike Jane Austen's narrator, when they use words like truth, they are not being ironic. Many early authorial narrators make judgements about the world that readers were supposed to accept as true. In his description of Squire Allworthy in *Tom Jones*, for example, Fielding's narrator tells us that 'nature' had bestowed on him, 'an agreeable person, a sound constitution, a solid understanding, and a benevolent heart'; while Allworthy's sister 'was of that species of women whom you commend rather for good qualities than beauty' (p.19). Judgements of this kind, when they come from a 'godlike' anonymous narrator, tend to make modern readers uneasy. In the early years of the novel – in the eighteenth and nineteenth century – people tended to make sweeping assumptions about issues relating to what has value and what is natural; they assumed everyone knew what was meant when they spoke of those things, and felt the same way. The way that novels were written simply reflects that kind of thinking. These days, however, we are less sure of ourselves: we are less certain that we know what constitutes value, or what is natural, and we are less keen on voices claiming authority in those areas. So when Fielding's narrator tells us that Allworthy is worthy, we might be inclined to ask, by what criteria is he being judged? The same goes for his sister's 'good qualities', not to mention her lack of 'beauty'. In the early days of the novel most readers were disinclined to ask such questions, assuming that values are universal, rather than contingent and culturally relative.

Modern and Modernist Narrators

David Lodge writes in *The Art of Fiction* (1992) that, 'Modern fiction has tended to suppress or eliminate the authorial voice, by presenting action through the consciousness of the characters or by handing over to them the narrative task itself.'[17] He is referring to the fact that the twentieth century saw an increasing preference for first-person narrators, or third-person narrators who are only prepared to *show* the story, rather than comment on or evaluate it. The modern approach tends to utilise detached narrators who present situations without evaluation, or narratives that filter everything through the consciousness of characters, limiting the reader's knowledge of a scene to that of the character itself. The emergence of such strategies is often associated with modernism, a cultural phenomenon of the early twentieth century that, among other things, sought to challenge assumptions about how the world could or should be represented in art.

There is some evidence of this more circumscribed approach to storytelling in James Joyce's short story collection, *Dubliners* (1914). Many of these stories are told in the third person, but the narrator tends to be neutral – it does not evaluate the characters or tell us what to think. So in a story like 'Eveline', an extradiegetic narrative voice is present, but it often merges with Eveline's voice in a way that closes the gap between the narrator and the character. Consider these lines from the beginning of the story:

> Few people passed. The man out of the last house passed on his way home; she heard his footsteps clacking along the concrete pavement and afterwards crunching on the cinder path before the new red houses. One time there used to be a field there in which

---

[17] David Lodge, *The Art of Fiction* (London: Penguin, 1992) p.10

they used to play every evening with other people's children. Then a man from Belfast bought the field and built houses in it – not like their little brown houses, but bright brick houses with shining roofs.[18]

The external narrator is clearly evident in the first sentence, but notice how the narrative appears to shape itself around the character's perception: words like 'clacking' and 'crunching' convey Eveline's sense impressions, and eventually the voice seems to become hers. It mirrors the kind of language Eveline might have used as a younger girl, for instance, with phrases such as 'little brown houses'.

In this story Eveline wants to start a new life, but she's too scared to because she is bound by conventional ways of thinking; the narrator doesn't tell us this, he reveals it via the way Eveline speaks, thinks and acts. For instance, we are shown Eveline holding on to letters she had written to her family – suggesting an inability to let go of the past – and we see her praying, taking comfort in ritual and routine. Most importantly, when she decides to stay rather than leave, we have to make up our own minds about whether Eveline is doing the right thing.

An approach to storytelling which puts a character's consciousness squarely at the centre of the narration can be seen in Joyce's first novel, *A Portrait of the Artist as a Young Man* (1916). Here the author's hero, Stephen Dedalus, is himself a developing writer; he states Joyce's own aesthetic in simple terms:

---

[18] James Joyce, 'Eveline' in *The Essential James Joyce* (London: Panther Books, 1985; *Dubliners* first published, 1914) p.40

> The artist, like the God of the creation, remains within or behind or beyond or above his handiwork, invisible, refined out of existence, indifferent, paring his fingernails.[19]

In this novel virtually everything is seen from Stephen's perspective and the distance between the narrator and the focaliser seems to collapse; apart from a short extract from Stephen's diary, the narrative is presented in the third rather than first person, but the presence of an extradiegetic narrator is often hard to detect, and we are given no point of reference from which to judge Stephen. We are basically presented with Stephen's consciousness, and everything is filtered through that with minimal mediation. The nature of the language employed in the narrative reflects the steps in Stephen's intellectual maturation, beginning with the childlike simplicity of his first recollections, and gradually becoming more sophisticated. This is the famous opening to the novel:

> Once upon a time and a very good time it was there was a moocow coming down along the road and this moocow that was coming down along the road met a nicens little boy named baby tuckoo.
>
> His father told him that story: his father looked at him through a glass: he had a hairy face.
>
> He was baby tuckoo. The moocow came down the road where Betty Byrne lived: she sold lemon platt (p.176).

The opening takes the form of a collection of sense-

---

[19] James Joyce, *A Portrait of the Artist as a Young Man* in *The Essential James Joyce* (London: Panther Books, 1985; novel first published, 1916). All future references will be to this edition.

impressions: the things he has seen as an infant, such as his bearded father looking at him, the words he has heard, such as 'moocow', and the things he has tasted such as 'lemon platt'; as the passage develops it goes on to refer to other sense-impressions such as his experience of wetting the bed, and snatches of songs he half remembers. But notice that, while there is a reference to 'once upon a time' in the opening sentence, we are not actually told when this took place; indeed there is nothing in the way of contextualisation: we do not know who is speaking or where or when. We might normally expect to get this contextualisation from the narrator, but Joyce forgoes it in order to place us inside the child's mind with as little mediation as possible from any external narrative voice. As the story progresses, Joyce continues to present the perceptions and impressions of the child's mind, without attempting to connect them the way a conventional narrator would: readers are forced to work out these connections for themselves, and in this way we gradually get to know the protagonist.

Joyce takes the focus on a single consciousness a stage further in *Ulysses* (1922), which is generally regarded as a seminal work in the development of the novel. It focuses on a day in the life of Leopold Bloom as he wanders around Dublin on 16 June 1904. Bloom's wife Molly also features, as does Stephen Dedalus, the hero of *Portrait*. As the title suggests, the novel alludes to Homer's story of Odysseus (called Ulysses in Roman myth) and his travels and adventures on his journey home from war. This structure gives Bloom's apparently mundane experiences a mythical dimension. The principal narrative strategy in the novel is often termed stream of consciousness. We are given intimate insights into the characters' thoughts, regardless of how trivial and private; it presents subjective, sensory impressions of reality, unmediated by a narrator, and our sense of the characters' world is created less as a result of a narrator telling us about it, and more via the characters' interaction with it. Consider this passage conveyed from Bloom's perspective:

> A cloud began to cover the sun slowly, wholly. Grey. Far.
>
> No, not like that. A barren land, bare waste. Vulcanic lake, the dead sea: no fish, weedless, sunk deep in the earth. No wind could lift those waves, grey metal, poisonous foggy waters. Brimstone they called it raining down: the cities of the plain: Sodom, Gomorrah, Edom. All dead names. A dead sea in a dead land, grey and old. Old now. It bore the oldest, the first race. A bent hag crossed from Cassidy's, clutching a naggin bottle by the neck. The oldest people. Wandered far away over all the earth, captivity by captivity, multiplying, dying, being born everywhere. It lay there now. Now it could bear no more. Dead: an old woman's: the grey sunken cunt of the world.
>
> Desolation.[20]

Bloom is feeling depressed, and his thoughts mirror that experience. A cloud covers the sun and he begins to think of desolation and death. His thoughts turn to the Dead Sea and then, following the Biblical connotations of this, to Sodom

---

[20] Quoted in Paul Schwaber, *The Cast of Characters: A Reading of* Ulysses (Yale: Yale University Press, 1999) p.87

and Gomorrah: in other words, the thoughts are associative; the connections are implicit. These references are woven into Bloom's impressions of Dublin life, suggested by the image of an old woman crossing the road, clutching a bottle.

Another term related to stream of consciousness is interior monologue; this is often regarded as a sub-category of stream of consciousness. It refers to sensory impressions that are presented in the form of a monologue: in other words, they are presented directly by the character. So the opening of *A Portrait of the Artist* could legitimately be called a stream of consciousness, but most critics would not use the term interior monologue. The term is usually reserved for long passages, and one of the most famous is Molly Bloom's soliloquy, the poetic monologue from Bloom's wife which closes *Ulysses*:

> I was a Flower of the mountain yes when I put the rose in my hair like the Andalusian girls used or shall I wear a red yes and how he kissed me under the Moorish wall and I thought well as well him as another and then I asked him with my eyes to ask again yes and then he asked me would I yes to say yes my mountain flower and first I put my arms around him yes and drew him down to me so he could feel my breasts all perfume yes and his heart was going like mad and yes I said yes I will Yes.[21]

These are the final lines of the soliloquy, which in its entirety is over forty pages long. Molly has been having an affair with a man called Blazes Boylan, but here has accepted her husband Leopold back in her bed after his day of

---

[21] James Joyce, *Ulysses* (London: Urban Romatics, 2013. First published, 1922) p. 656

wandering. Bloom's return to Molly is supposed to reflect Odysseus' return to Penelope at the end of Homer's *Odyssey*. Up to this stage in the soliloquy she has spent much time reminiscing about her life, her various sexual encounters with other men, arguments she's had with Bloom, among other things, but now in the final lines her thoughts focus on her connection with her husband. Notice how her thoughts come in a rush – there are hardly any sentence breaks in the whole soliloquy, which consists of only eight sentences in total, and there is no punctuation. The thoughts merge together, emulating the way such thoughts might occur to us in reality. Molly's sense impressions mingle with specific memories of her first sexual encounter with Leopold Bloom: she remembers herself as a mountain flower with perfumed breasts, and the rhythm of the language, with the reiteration of the word *yes*, mirrors the passion she experienced.

Postmodern Narrators

Narrators who draw attention to the storytelling process have been a feature of narrative fiction for centuries. As seen above, in the eighteenth century, Laurence Sterne in *Tristram Shandy* has his narrator comment on his own story in a variety of ways, even constructing debates with imaginary readers about the manner in which he is presenting his tale. Narratives which lay bare their storytelling techniques, or that foreground their fictional status, are sometimes called self-conscious fictions or metafictions. Consider this passage from John Barth's short story 'Lost in the Funhouse' (1968).

> Ambrose was 'at that awkward age'. His voice came out high-pitched as a child's if he let himself get carried away; to be on the safe side, therefore, he moved and spoke with *deliberate calm* and *adult gravity*. Talking soberly of unimportant or irrelevant matters and listening consciously to the sound of your own voice are useful habits for maintaining control in this difficult interval. *En route* to Ocean City he sat in the back seat of the family car with his brother Peter, age fifteen, and Magda G —, age fourteen, a pretty girl and exquisite young lady, who lived not far from them on B — Street in the town of D —, Maryland. Initials, blanks, or both were often substituted for proper names in nineteenth-century fiction to enhance the illusion of reality. It is as if the author felt it necessary to delete the names for reasons of tact or legal liability. Interestingly, as with other aspects of realism, it is an *illusion* that is being enhanced, by purely artificial means. Is it likely, does it violate the principle of verisimilitude, that a thirteen-year-old boy could make such a sophisticated observation? A girl of fourteen is *the psychological coeval* of a boy of fifteen or sixteen; a thirteen-year-old boy, therefore, even one precocious in some other respects, might be three years *her emotional junior*.[22]

---

[22] John Barth, 'Lost in the Funhouse' in A. Walton, ed. *Major American Short Stories* (New York and Oxford: Oxford University Press, 1994; first collected in Barth's story collection, *Lost in the Funhouse*, 1968) p.691

Notice how the extradiegetic-heterodiegetic narrator makes reference to how writers traditionally create the 'illusion of reality' – he is overtly referencing the tools of the storyteller's art, and in so doing draws attention to the fact that his own narrative is fictional; he implies that it is an illusion to think that stories offer a window on reality. He also raises the issue of his own fallibility as a narrator, asking if the claims he makes about his character are believable, or whether they are at odds with 'the principle of verisimilitude'. The narrator continues in this vein throughout the story, questioning the possibility of realism and notion of truth in fiction. The idea of originality also seems to be at issue: for instance the narrator is very aware of cliché, using a stock phrase to describe Ambrose's condition – 'that awkward age' – which suggests that the theme of the story itself might be a little well-worn. It turns out to be a coming-of-age story, focusing on the maturation of a sensitive adolescent, and the narrator seems to want to signal that he's aware his theme is something of an old chestnut for writers.

Narratives exhibiting characteristics of this kind became much more common in the late twentieth century. In an essay called 'The Literature of Exhaustion' (1967) John Barth suggests that it's to do with the 'used-upness' of available fictional 'forms' and 'possibilities'; the implication is that writers are running out of plots, styles, and available modes of expression; there is a crisis of originality, and the prevalence of self-consciousness in narrative is a response to what Barth called, 'the felt exhaustion of certain possibilities' for writers in the modern world.[23] There was also an increasing awareness among many writers of the limits of language as a mode of communication. The work of Poststructuralist theorists such as Jacques Derrida and Roland Barthes follows from the premise that language is an abstract system of signs that has no fixed relationship with reality: the idea that it can put people in touch with truth or reality is a fallacy. Many narratives in the late twentieth century seem to want to signal the limits of linguistic communication: to acknowledge the impossibility of truth or certainty in narrative. Preoccupations of this kind are indicative of Postmodernist fiction which tends to be characterised by doubt and relativism; Postmodernists feel that there are no certainties, and the proliferation of self-conscious, ironic narratives reflects a desire to make this point.

We saw how Modernist narrators like Joyce's suggest a reluctance to assume the God-like, all-knowing perspective of the early omniscient narrators, but Postmodernists like John Barth, and many more who follow him, seem even less willing to make claims about the world. They produce narratives that refuse to take themselves seriously and often go to considerable lengths to undermine their own assertions. The fictions of writers such as Martin Amis, Angela Carter, E.L. Doctorow, Umberto Eco, and Philip Roth frequently exhibit a patina of irony that keeps a sense of the story's artificiality constantly in mind. This irony is not always created by narrative intrusions into the text (as with Barth above),

---

[23] John Barth 'The Literature of Exhaustion' in *The Friday Book: Essays and Other Non-Fiction* (London: The John Hopkins University Press, 1984. Originally published 1967) p.64

but often by less direct means such as the self-conscious referencing of other stories (sometimes referred to as intertextuality), the incorporation of overt stereotype, or of clearly fictionalised versions of real events, and so on. For instance, Philip Roth's novel *The Human Stain* (2000) is narrated by a fictional author, Nathan Zuckerman; he has been asked to write the life story of a man, Coleman Silk, who feels he has been wronged by the college at which he once taught, and persecuted by an ex-colleague, Delphine Roux. Readers are never allowed forget that they are being offered an author's version of Coleman's life, rather than the so-called truth. Sometimes Zuckerman is like a conventional first-person narrator relating his various encounters with Coleman, sometimes he is more like an extradiegetic-heterodiegetic narrator telling Coleman's story in the third person. Not only is Zuckerman's status as an author constantly referenced, but his narrative is shown to be partly artificial – for instance, the names of the characters and the locations allude to classical mythology in a way that foregrounds the notion of mythmaking and storytelling throughout; likewise, the novel's structure reflects the five acts of classical drama. There is a good reason why the novel constantly asserts its fictional status – one of its themes has to do with the dangers of certainty and the idea that there is only one way of looking at the world. Coleman is victimized by a woman who thinks she knows how people should behave, and who despises Coleman because he contravenes her ideals. Her name, Delphine, ironically references Delphi, the home of the Oracle (the font of all knowledge in classical mythology). The novel seeks to expose her assumptions as pernicious, suggesting the inevitability of uncertainty: the narrative underscores this point by constantly stressing the subjectivity and fallibility of its own assertions; the implication being that all narratives, whether fictional or non-fictional can never really articulate truth.

Another interesting example of such self-consciousness can be found in David Lodge's *Nice Work* (1988). In this novel Lodge employs a type of omniscient narrator that at first sight wouldn't be out of place in a nineteenth-century novel: the narrator knows everything about the characters, commenting on and evaluating them in ways that occasionally seem a little out-of-place in contemporary fiction. The story focuses on the relationship between a young literature lecturer, Robyn Penrose, and a Midlands factory manager, Vic Wilcox. Robyn's field of expertise is the nineteenth-century novel, and the story is littered with references to classic novels of the industrial genre; for instance, every chapter is prefaced with an extract from nineteenth-century industrial novels such as Dickens's *Hard Times* (1854), Benjamin Disraeli's *Sybil* (1845), among others. As the story develops it becomes clear that *Nice Work* is something of a pastiche of this genre, most notably of Elizabeth Gaskell's novel, *North and South* (1855). The style and the themes of this novel are referenced, and Lodge mirrors them in his own story to some degree. Robyn and Vic are from different backgrounds and have antithetical outlooks on life: she is a left-wing academic, he is a hardnosed conservative. They are thrown together in the fictional Midlands town of Rummidge thanks to a government scheme designed to give academics an insight into the world of industry. To some extent this mirrors the plot of *North and South*, where Gaskell's Margaret Hale must move to the industrial Midlands where she is forced into contact with the wealthy manufacturer John Thornton. As with Margaret and John, Robyn and Vic initially repel one another, but a mutual respect and fondness develops. One common device in nineteenth-century novels is the use of legacies as a means of freeing the characters – particularly women – from poverty. This is a device that Robyn criticises because it suggests women's dependence on the hand of fate, but it is another plot theme that *Nice Work* self-consciously utilises when Robyn herself receives a legacy that provides a happy ending for both herself and Vic. In other words, *Nice Work* is an example of a narrative that employs cliché in an ironic way: by overtly signalling its indebtedness to the industrial novel genre it legitimises the reuse of outmoded styles and themes; Lodge brings them to bear on the Midlands of the 1980s, and they offer an appropriate parallel to the ideological conflicts that raged at the height of Thatcherism.

Narrative and Viewpoint Issues for Creative Writers

As David Lodge has written, 'The choice of point(s) of view from which the story is told is arguably the most important single decision that the novelist has to make' (*Art of Fiction*, p.26) This is the case because, as seen above, the issue of narration and focalisation can have a profound effect on a reader's experience of the story and how they relate to the characters on moral and emotional levels. Obviously, the viewpoint will be determined by the kind of story a writer is seeking to tell: whether the story focuses principally on a single or multiple characters; whether it weaves together several stories that necessitate shifts in place and time, and so on. Most fledgling writers find it easier to write in the first person than in the third. For one thing it feels more natural as a storytelling style; it is more straightforward too because, with only one viewpoint to worry about, it is easier for writers to stay in control of perspective. It helps keep a narrative focused and integrated. Also, there is a potential intensity and intimacy associated with the first person: as suggested above, it is possible to address the reader directly and establish more of a bond between narrator and reader. There are potential problems with the first person of course: one has to do with the fact that it is very restrictive. First-person character-narrators can only really relate what they experience for themselves, or what's related to them by other characters; also they cannot offer access to any other character's thoughts or feelings. Writers can get around this by having more than one first-person narrator, and then by moving from one character-narrator to another. For instance, novels such as Andrea Levi's *Small Island* (2004) and Laura Hird's *Born Free* (1999) do this: they have a number of first-person narrators who tell the story from their own perspective, passing the narrative baton as the story proceeds. Irvine Welsh's *Trainspotting* (1993) does something similar, moving between character-narrators and adopting different voices to create a patchwork of perspectives that together create the story. A more common way of getting around this problem, of course, is to use a third-person narrator.

Third-person narrators offer much more flexibility, as they can vary how they narrate the story by employing varying degrees of omniscience. A fully omniscient narrator can take the God-like perspective, moving in and out of characters' minds at will, commenting on any aspect of the story – including events happening offstage or events that have yet to happen. A disadvantage of using narrators that give full reign to omniscience is that it can prove hard to stay in control of the perspective: shifts of focalisation mid-scene, for instance, can disorientate readers and undermine their connection with the fictional world. At the other extreme, third-person narrators can choose to limit the viewpoint to external focalisation. For instance, Ernest Hemingway's short story 'The Killers' is presented almost exclusively in dialogue; the perspective is entirely external and readers have no access to the thoughts of the characters; it is one of the purest examples of showing rather than telling, and readers must draw their own conclusions about the implications of the scene they are offered. A disadvantage here is that it can have the effect of distancing the characters from the reader, making it difficult for them to emotionally engage.

It is much more common for third-person narrators to employ internal focalisation, but to restrict this to one or two characters who tend to be the main protagonists in a story. When choosing the point-of-view characters some thought obviously needs to be given to which characters have the biggest stake in the story, and which will offer the most compelling perspective(s). It is occasionally said that unsympathetic characters do not make good point-of-view characters because people find it hard to share the perspective of people they don't like. It is difficult to give credence to this given the spectacular success of novels with paedophiles and serial killers as sustained viewpoint characters (Vladimir Nabokov's Humbert Humbert; Bret Easton Ellis's Patrick Bateman); their success probably suggests that reader engagement and identification has less to do with the viewpoint character's likeability than with their capacity to be interesting: a very obvious prerequisite of successful storytelling that is often overlooked. It is also sometimes suggested that writers should refrain from employing sustained-viewpoint characters who die or disappear partway through the narrative. Again, this depends on the story in question; skilful authors can exploit our emotional identification with viewpoint characters in order to augment the emotional impact of their demise. Catherine O'Flynn does this to great effect, for instance, in her 2007 novel, *What Was Lost*. For the first quarter of the book the viewpoint character is a ten-year-old girl called Kate; when Kate suddenly vanishes, the fact that the reader has been intimately involved with her makes this disappearance a more traumatic and moving experience. David Nicholls creates a similar effect in his novel *One Day* (2009). The sudden and unexpected death of Emma is rendered all the more shocking and poignant because she has been one of two principal viewpoint characters for much of the story.

Characters

The notion of character is a complex one; indeed, the extent to which it is even legitimate to talk about character in narrative is a source of debate. In narratology the term has tended to denote a textual construct akin to a human being: characters in stories are, for want of a better phrase, fictional people. Ostensibly this seems harmless enough – individuals outside stories are often thought of as having defining traits: they have an appearance and a personality that distinguishes them from others; they have names that can be attached to a set of characteristics that apparently describe and define them. But to what extent *do* people have stable or irreducible characters? In the early twentieth century Virginia Woolf made the point that individuals in the real world seem to be constantly in a state of flux, rather than fixed entities: what we refer to as their 'character' is always changing; more recently writers like Hélène Cixous have suggested that the 'I' is more like a collection of selves, as opposed to a single, integrated self. In his novel *The Counterlife* (1986) Philip Roth dramatizes this notion of self, and eloquently expresses it via his protagonist Nathan Zuckerman:

> Being Zuckerman is one long performance and the very opposite of what is thought of as being oneself. In fact, those who most seem to be themselves appear to me people impersonating what they think they might like to be, believe they ought to be, or wish to be taken to be ... if there even is a natural being, an irreducible self, it is rather small, I think, and may even be the root of all impersonation ... All I can tell

> you with certainty is that I, for one, have no self ... What I have instead are a variety of impersonations I can do, and not only of myself – a troupe of players that I have internalized, a permanent company of actors I can call on when a self is required.[24]

Clearly this is at odds with traditional notions of character as an integrated and irreducible thing; as Rimmon-Kenan says, 'If the self is a constant flux or if it is a "group acting together", the concept of character changes or disappears, the "old stable ego" disintegrates' (*Narrative Fiction*, p.30). This raises questions about the meaning of the term character in the real world (i.e. as applied to real people), and has obvious implications as to how we might interpret character in narrative. Traditional literary criticism tended to evaluate characters in terms of consistency, motivation, and plausibility, but if it is no longer possible to think of real-life individuals as stable or predictable, how can these criteria be applied with any degree of legitimacy to their fictional counterparts? How can the idea of an alternating 'troupe of players' be squared with the notion of consistency? How does the concept of motivation relate to the concept of the self as a performer? If a character is a collection of selves, then which is the plausible self?

---

[24] Philip Roth, *The Counterlife* (New York: Farrar, Straus and Giroux, 1987) pp.319-321

Are Fictional Characters Like People?

The idea of fictional characters being like people might sound strange – after all, characters are created by words and do not really exist – but there has been much debate about the viability of fictional characters beyond the narratives that construct them. On the one hand, there are semiotic theories of character which stress the character's dependence on text; on the other hand, there are so-called mimetic theories which consider the text as a reflection of reality, and evaluate character in the way we might evaluate real people. A theorist like Roland Barthes would fall into the first category. In his book *S/Z* (1970) he challenges the concept of realism by showing how texts communicate via a network of codes; he considers character to be associated with what he calls 'the semic code', arguing that they are shaped by the interplay of 'semes' – signifiers which suggest traits that, though linked to the character's name in a text, in no sense approximate to a real person. In his analysis of Honoré de Balzac's novella *Sarrasine*, Barthes cites Sarrasine's habit of whittling on a pew during church services as an indication of impiety, while his habit of writing on the walls suggests an anti-social nature, and so on. Each seme has connotations which cumulatively produce our impression of a character; however, inevitably some semes are unstable and deny the possibility of a fixed meaning; for example, according to Barthes, the 'e' at the end of Sarrasine's name suggests femininity in French, and because femininity is an ambiguous signifier whose meaning can never be reduced to one thing, Sarrasine can never be reduced either: he, like all characters, is never stable but invariably shifting along with the connotations of the semes from which he is constructed. There is no point talking about characters as representations of reality, then, because their relationship with the world outside the text is perpetually in flux.

As suggested, however, there are critics who are happy to detach characters from their textual moorings and subject them to the kind of analyses applied to real people: anthropological, psychoanalytical, sociological, and so on. Certainly the idea that characters cannot exist outside a narrative seems rather reductive, and is at odds with the experience of reading and discussing fiction. It is worth recalling the distinction between narrative and story made earlier: while in the first instance characters are products of the narrative in which they appear, they also feature at the level of the story which, as we have seen, can be abstracted from the narrative. For instance, a reader of *The Great Gatsby* will have images of Gatsby, Nick, Tom and Daisy in mind, and a general understanding of their character, without necessarily remembering any of the words (or indeed semes) employed to create them. Clearly they have sufficient presence and viability outside the text for critics to discuss them as, among other things, representative of attitudes and types current in early twentieth-century American society, and even as incarnations of real people (it's said for instance that Daisy is modelled on the American socialite Ginevra King). It seems legitimate to many readers that fictional characters should be invoked in discussions and analyses of history and culture, and with reference to the human condition in general.

Character or Plot?

The relationship between character and plot has also been the subject of debate among theorists. In his book *Poetics* Aristotle said, 'tragedy is an imitation, not of men, but of an action and of life, and life consists in action.'[25] In other words, Aristotle implies that character is subordinate to plot; character is present in narrative only in order to serve the plot. This is a view shared by formulists like Vladímir Propp, mentioned earlier; for him characters can be understood in relation to the functions they have in the scheme of the story. He identified the following recurring character types in the folk tales he analysed:

- *The Hero* – who can also take the form of victim.
- *The Villain* – that character who is in conflict with the hero.
- *The Dispatcher* – the character who sends the hero off on his mission. Sometimes this is the princess's father who sends the hero on a quest.
- *The Helper* – the one who helps the hero, often via magic.
- *The Princess* – on occasion she is the object of the hero's mission (if he needs to rescue her), or sometimes his quest will involve her hand in marriage as a prize.
- *The Princess's Father* – sometimes functions to give the task to the hero.
- *The Donor* – the one who prepares the hero for the

---

[25] Aristotle, *Poetics*, in S.H. Butcher, trans., *Aristotle's Theory of Poetry and Fine Art* (New York: Dover, 1951) p.27

mission, and who often gives the hero some magical object.

• *The False Hero* – the character who can initially take the glory for the hero's actions; he can sometimes have designs on the princess.

Notice how these characters relate to actions in the story – they all have a role that contributes to the plot. Versions of Propp's types can be seen in other narratives, of course, not just folk tales; just to take one example from contemporary fiction, the key cast of the Harry Potter stories might break down in the following way: Hero=Harry Potter; Villain=Voldemort; The Donor=Dumbledore; Dispatcher=Hagrid; Helper=Ron/Hermione; The False Hero=Draco Malfoy/Professor Quirrel. The roles of some characters change and overlap somewhat, of course, particularly over the entire series of books, and there isn't really a Princess as such, although the latter role might be said to equate to the possibility of Harry's freedom, and that of his allies.

Some critics privilege plot over character, then, but others insist on the importance of character. The American novelist Henry James, for instance, said 'What is character but the determination of incident? What is incident but the illustration of character?'[26] In other words, it is difficult to conceive of significant action in a narrative except in relation to how it impacts on character. While the idea of characters

---

[26] Henry James, 'The Art of Fiction', in Morris Shapira, (ed.) *Henry James: Selected Literary Criticism* (Harmondsworth: Penguin, 1963; originally published 1884) p.30

being subordinate to action might work in relation to fairy tales, it seems less satisfactory when applied to novels where characters play a substantial role, and effectively dominate the plot. Many of James's own novels – such as *The Portrait of a Lady* (1881) and *The Wings of the Dove* (1902) – are good examples of stories which focus on the meticulous delineation of character, and in which characters have primacy. Occasionally, critics make distinctions between plot-driven and character-driven stories, but they are hard to formally categorise in these simple terms.

Types of Character

Obviously, when we read a novel some characters feature more extensively than others; they are more substantial than others, more fully realised. There are major characters and there are minor characters: some are central to the story, others peripheral. In *Aspects of the Novel* E.M. Forster made a famous distinction between so-called flat characters and round characters. Flat characters for Forster are those that are 'constructed around a single idea or quality'; they tend to be defined by a single trait, a single characteristic. Flat characters, he argued, can be 'expressed in one sentence' (*Aspects*, p.75). They tend not to develop throughout the course of the story, and are sometimes referred to as static characters as a result; they're often stereotypes or caricatures, less layered and multifaceted than the more substantial characters. Round characters by contrast are multi-layered; they have greater complexity and variegation than flat characters. Consequently, whereas it's possible to sum up a flat character in a single sentence, this is less easy with round characters. In a novel like *Wuthering Heights*, characters such as Lockwood and Joseph could be called flat, while Heathcliff and Catherine are more rounded. In *Pride and Prejudice*, Mr Collins is flat; Elizabeth Bennett and Fitzwilliam Darcy are round. In *The Great Gatsby*, George and Myrtle Wilson are flat; Nick Carraway and Jay Gatsby are round. Round characters tend to be the central characters, then; very often they are the protagonists of the book. We get an insight into what motivates them, we learn a lot about their attitudes, prejudices and preoccupations; and they also develop as characters as the story progresses. So, for instance, in the case of Nick Carraway we see how his exposure to the excesses of East Coast life contributes to his maturation, and his decision to relocate himself in an environment more conducive to the kind of moral life he comes to value.

There are a few problems with Forster's distinction. Firstly, the term flat suggests two-dimensionality and stasis, but many characters that Forster would define as flat for these reasons aren't two-dimensional or static at all. A number of Charles Dickens's so-called caricatures, for instance, are some of the most vivid characters in the history of fiction. They may not *develop* as characters and they may not have psychological depth, but they're not two-dimensional; they're very much three-dimensional. Also, the distinction between flat and round is rather polarising: it is reductive, and doesn't allow for middle ground. There are numerous characters who are neither round nor flat in Forster's terms. So, in *The Great Gatsby*, do Daisy and Tom Buchanan fall into the category of round or flat? In some respects they are meant to reflect attitudes that Fitzgerald discerned in his social milieu, and thus are types in this sense, but they also have considerable substance. Daisy in particular could be called multidimensional: she demonstrates what appear to be genuine feelings for Gatsby which are indicative of a capacity to love; this conflicts with her fickleness and disloyalty, of course, and augments our sense of her complexity. Also, sometimes in fiction you get characters who are multifaceted and substantial, and yet do not really develop or grow as characters. Indeed, the very fact that a character *doesn't* develop might be a characteristic that allows us to define them as more complex. Rimmon-Kenan makes the point that Miss Havisham in *Great Expectations* fails to develop as a character, but this is not because she is flat; rather it is because she suffered the trauma of being jilted by the man who was due to marry her, and this has arrested her development. So, in a sense, the very fact that she fails to develop tells us something about her as a character that increases our impression of her complexity, and roundness.

Despite the inadequacy of this terminology, the terms flat and round are still used in the discussion of characters in academic criticism. They are also applied to characters in an evaluative way, of course. Round is used to praise an author's creation as convincing, and flat is employed disapprovingly. While flat characters – particularly caricatures – can be vivid, entertaining and memorable, it is often suggested that only round characters can offer the degree of emotional engagement required to move readers significantly. Stories, particularly novels, obviously employ a combination of both; certainly it was Forster's view that the intermingling of round and flat characters is reflective of the lived experience, and so serious work should strive to achieve this.

Characterisation

The term characterisation is used to refer to the methods narrators use to delineate a character. We can divide this into two broad types of character construction: direct definition, and indirect presentation.

Direct Definition

Direct definition explicitly names a trait or characteristic that a character is supposed to have – in other words, a narrator tells the reader what a character is like. An example of direct definition in David Lodge's *Nice Work*, for instance, comes when the narrator says of Robyn Penrose: 'She seems to have ordinary human feelings, ambitions, desires, to suffer anxieties, frustrations, fears, like anyone else in this imperfect world, and to have a natural inclination to try and make it a better place.'[27] This character has an innate social conscience:

---

[27] David Lodge, *Nice Work* (London: Vintage, 2011; first published 1989) p.22

we don't have to infer that she wants to make the world a better place because we are told directly that this is how we are meant to think of her. Direct definition only really counts if it comes from the most authoritative voice in the text. In *Nice Work* the most authoritative voice is the extradiegetic-heterodiegetic narrator who knows everything about the characters; if a character assessment comes from somewhere else – i.e. from the perspective of another character in a story – then the reader cannot trust it in the same way. This is also the case when characters tell the reader about themselves, a device sometimes called self-characterisation: clearly this should be treated with scepticism because there is always a possibility of unreliability.

Indirect Presentation

The second type, indirect presentation, doesn't mention a trait explicitly but has it revealed or displayed in some way, and the reader must infer what the character is like. Characters can be revealed indirectly to us in four principal ways: through action, speech, appearance and environment. In other words: through what they do, what they say, how they look, and where they reside.

Action

A character can be revealed via what they do, of course, but some actions are more significant than others in this respect. If a character takes a shower in the morning, this doesn't necessarily tell us much about them; but if they take twenty showers throughout the day, this might. In Lodge's *Nice Work,* Victor Wilcox reads *The Times*, while Robyn Penrose reads the *Guardian*. This reveals something about them. As a *Times* reader Vic is intelligent, but with a conservative orientation; as a *Guardian* reader Robyn is also intelligent, but with a leaning toward the political left. When Vic has a shave we are told he uses a British razor – this tells us something too: he's patriotic, and wants to do what he can to support the British economy. He believes fervently enough in this to disparage his son for using a French disposable razor. Vic is willing to put himself out in order to do something positive for his country, which is a significant characteristic.

Speech

Scott Fitzgerald's Jay Gatsby refers to people as 'sport' in various conversations, and this is a defining trait that helps form our impression of him. It appears as an affectation, at odds with other aspects of his personality. The more he is shown doing it the more suspicious it makes us feel: it augments our sense of his potential dubiousness. Eventually we learn that Gatsby is trying hard to present himself as an

Oxford-educated gentleman, as a product of a world to which he has never belonged. This speech affectation helps create a sense of who Gatsby is as a character: someone who presents himself as 'great', but whose pretensions are undermined by reality.

Appearance

External appearance is also used to delineate character. This can include aspects of appearance that people have control over, such as what they wear, and those they don't have control over, such as their physical features. Dora and Nora in Carter's *Wise Children* dress the same at seventy-five as they did when they were young women. They still wear the same make-up, and too much of it. This suggests that they identify strongly with a particular period in their lives; ordinarily there might be a degree of sadness about this, but that is not the case here. The twins are self-aware enough to acknowledge that they dress in an inappropriate way, and there's something endearing about their defiant determination not to grow old gracefully; it bolsters our sense of their eccentricity, and their strength of character.

While characters usually have control over what they wear, they cannot help the physical aspects of their appearance, yet this too can be used to suggest character traits. In the early days of the novel many people assumed that there was a scientific basis for a relationship between physical appearance and character – the Swiss physiognomist Johann Lavater

(1741-1801) was influential in this field. While scientific theories linking appearance and character were discredited long ago, some authors still use a character's physical appearance to imply character traits. Victor in *Nice Work*, for instance, is only five feet five and it is often suggested, wrongly, that shortness in stature is linked to an aggressive, driven personality. However, Victor Wilcox *does* conform to this idea: he is a pugnacious, aggressive character, and thus his physical appearance helps bolster this aspect of his character in the mind of the reader.

Environment

Environment can tell us something about character as well. The narrator of Lodge's *Nice Work* goes to some lengths to describe the interior of Robyn Penrose's house, for instance:

> There are books and periodicals everywhere – on the shelves on the tables, on the floor – posters and reproductions of modern paintings on the walls, parched-looking pot plants in the fireplace ... Robyn picks her way across the floor [walking] between books, back numbers of *Critical Inquiry* and *Women's Review*, LP albums by Bach, Philip Glass and Phil Collins ... and the occasional wine glass or coffee cup, to the desk (*Nice Work*, pp.30-31).

We can tell a lot about Robyn from this. We're obviously meant to see the clutter of her environment as an indication of the kind of person she is and the kind of priorities she has. Mundane domestic tasks like tidying and washing up take second place to the life of the mind. Her intellectual pursuits take precedence over watering the plants too. Her tastes are reflected in the kind of things she chooses to have around her. They are refined, but they're also experimental and modern. She likes Bach, the Baroque composer, but also the avant-garde composer Philip Glass; at the same time she's familiar with popular 80s music: her choices combine to present her as someone who is simultaneously traditional and contemporary – a bit of a contradiction.

In Angela Carter's *Wise Children* Dora and Nora live in Brixton, on what Dora calls the 'wrong side of the tracks'. This location tells us something about the characters. In the past, Brixton wasn't the best part of London: it is not where the successful people live; and in financial terms, Dora and Nora haven't been successful either, so it is appropriate they should reside here. However, the wrong side of the tracks isn't necessarily all bad of course: there can be something colourful about it too – Brixton might not be Mayfair, but perhaps in some ways it's a bit more exciting; it has a kind of down-at-heel charm akin to that exhibited by these two characters.

Reinforcement: Analogy and Contrast

Our impression of a character can also be strengthened when narrators establish comparisons and differences between them and other things. For example, characters can have analogous names that work to suggest some aspect of their personalities, thereby reinforcing our sense of their fictional persona. Charles Dickens was known for this of course, with names like Uncle Pumblechook from *Great Expectations*: the syllables suggest 'puffed-up', which is indicative of his self-important character. In *Nice Work*, Lodge calls his heroine Robyn Penrose: Robyn is a modern Christian name for a modern woman – you don't get many women called Robyn before the 60s – so it's appropriate in this sense. Also, the name suggests a degree of gender ambiguity, and this is appropriate again as Robyn is a feminist who refuses to be confined by traditional gender expectations. Her surname is significant too; Penrose splits into two interesting syllables: pen is suggestive of writers and academics, and this again is suitable, while rose implies traditional notions of beauty. This is fitting too because, as the narrator tells us in a moment of direct definition, Robyn is 'comely'. As roses also have thorns, they're objects of beauty that insist on being treated with respect, like Robyn. Victor Wilcox is also an interesting name. Victor is a more traditional (old fashioned) name than Robyn. It suggests Victorian, and Victor *is* a bit of traditionalist. He finds Robyn outlandish when he first meets her; he's not sure whether he should approve of her. Victor also suggests winner, and he *is* something of a winner: he's a working-class man from fairly humble beginnings who has made a success of his life under Thatcherism. But his surname, Wilcox, suggests something different. It suggests wilting; it brings to mind the phrase 'wilting cock', implying impotence. This is in keeping with his character too because, as a middle-aged man, life is getting him down; when we first meet him his marriage is failing, his children are causing him difficulties, and there are problems at work. He's a winner, but he's also a bit of a loser, so again the connotations of his name are analogous to, or have similarities with, his character.

Also you can find analogies of other kinds in fiction. It's not unusual, particularly in pre-twentieth-century literature to find analogous landscape employed to underscore our sense of a character: a similarity between a character and the world they inhabit. Heathcliff in *Wuthering Heights*, for instance, is associated with the Yorkshire moors and there is an analogous relationship between his character and the nature of the moors: like them he is rugged and untamed.

The opposite of an analogy is a contrast, and contrasts can also work to reinforce our sense of character, only instead of working through similarity it works through difference. In Lodge's *Nice Work*, there is a contrast between the two central characters, Vic and Robyn. They have opposing personalities: the working-class, practical, traditional, conservative Vic is set against the middle-class, cerebral, feminist Robyn. In juxtaposition, the differences enhance our sense of them as individuals; the contrast throws their individual characteristics into relief.

Character Issues for Creative Writers

Characters are fundamental to fiction, of course, and writers need to work hard at delineating them convincingly. Characterisation has been discussed above, and writers can use the techniques of direct definition and indirect presentation listed there as a way of approaching character construction. It is generally considered preferable for the emphasis to be on indirect presentation as opposed to direct definition because the latter – particularly from an extradiegetic narrator – can seem reductive to the reader if it's not handled well: in other words, it is usually better to show rather than tell. If a narrator offers too much direct definition, then characters can become limited in the reader's mind to whatever they're defined as; for the most part it is preferable to reveal characters through what they do and what they say.

Readers want to visualise characters, but this doesn't mean that they need to be over-described visually: many writers consider it best to use succinct, significant details about how they appear. It is generally a good idea to make any crucial descriptive remarks early on in the story. When it comes to delineating key characters, readers quickly start developing images of characters and making assumptions about them, and it can be jarring if these are suddenly undermined part way through the reading experience; so it is probably not advisable to wait until page 150 to tell the reader that a central character has shocking pink hair and a wooden leg (unless, of course, you're deliberately withholding this information for the purpose of shock or suspense). It is often a good idea to name characters early on in the story too, not least because it helps readers locate them: a name offers something around which the various character indicators can assemble and cohere. It is worth putting a good deal of thought into names.

As seen above, names can be used to consolidate our sense of character; if you are stuck for a character's name then a phone book is a good place to look.

Somerset Maugham once said that as an author 'you can never know enough about your characters'[28], and many agree that it's a good idea for writers to develop an understanding of their main characters very early on in the creative process; indeed many invent substantial biographies for their characters before they even begin to write a novel: they may construct CVs for them, keep diaries for them written in character, and so on. Some writers need to feel that they know their characters' values and preoccupations as thoroughly as possible from the outset. While all of this information may not feature in the story, characters are more likely to have the patina of authenticity if an author has thought about them at length; certainly such writers will have more of a sense of how their characters might respond to given situations, and are perhaps less likely to have them do things that are, as it were, out of character.

When it comes to so-called literary fiction, it is also important to avoid stereotype and cliché: characters tend to be praised when they exhibit complexity, individuality and depth. This can be less of an issue in comedy, or in deliberately ironic fiction; arguably it is also less important in commercial and genre fiction, where readers seem more tolerant of character types. However, in all stories the most interesting characters are those who are conflicted; they are the characters

---

[28] Quoted in Sol Stein, *Stein on Writing* (New York: St Martin's Press, 1995) p.67

who are pulled in more than one direction: this is the case because it necessitates a character making decisions, which in turn generates suspense. As the novelist Stanley Elkin allegedly once said, 'I would never write about anyone who is not at the end of his rope'.[29]

Speech in Narrative

There are various ways in which the things characters say can be conveyed in narrative. They can, for instance, be paraphrased by the narrator, or summarised as in 'his conversation that day focused exclusively on football', which is known as diegetic summary. Alternatively, speech can be presented mimetically, as when a conversation is dramatised. Consider this dialogue from James Joyce's short story, 'The Dead':

> 'O, Mr Conroy,' said Lily to Gabriel when she opened the door for him, 'Miss Kate and Miss Julia thought you were never coming. Good-night, Mrs Conroy.'
> 'I'll engage they did,' said Gabriel, 'but they forget that my wife here takes three mortal hours to dress herself.'[30]

This is an example of direct speech: here the narrator is

---

[29] Quoted in Steven Lundin, *Peeking at Pillars: Quotes on Quotes on Writing* (Steven R. Lundin, 1995) p.29

[30] James Joyce, 'The Dead', in *The Essential James Joyce* (London: Panther Books, 1985; *Dubliners* first published, 1914) p.139. All future quotations are from this edition.

quoting what the characters are saying, making a clear distinction between their voices and the narrative voice. This gives the impression that the characters are conversing in real time. Now consider this passage from the same story:

> Kate and Julia came toddling down the dark stairs at once. Both of them kissed Gabriel's wife, said she must be perished alive and asked was Gabriel with her (p.139).

This is generally called indirect speech, where the speech of the character is reported by the narrator, rather than explicitly cited or bracketted off from the narrator's own discourse. There are no quotation marks, but the fact the speech belongs to a particular character is signalled by terms such as s/he said, s/he thought. Now compare that with another example from the same story:

> While she was threading her way back across the room Mrs Malins, without adverting to the interruption, went on to tell Gabriel what beautiful places there were in Scotland and beautiful scenery. Her son-in-law brought them every year to the lakes and they used to go fishing. Her son-in-law was a splendid fisher. One day he caught a beautiful big fish and the man in the hotel cooked it for their dinner (p.150).

There is no s/he said here, although the speech of a character is being suggested. The final sentence, for instance, with its use of phrases like 'beautiful big fish' and 'the man in the hotel', makes it evident that a voice other than that of the extradiegetic narrator is speaking: this voice has a simplicity and colloquial feel that the narrator's voice lacks; in a sense the narrator is going into character here, impersonating Mrs Malins's speech patterns. This is known as free indirect discourse, or free indirect style. Free indirect discourse is an important aspect of fiction that can create interesting levels of irony because of its capacity to, as it were, say two things at once. James Wood in *How Fiction Works*, for instance, says the following:

> Thanks to free indirect style, we see things through the character's eyes and language but also through the author's eyes and language, too. We inhabit omniscience and partiality at once. A gap opens up between author and character, and the bridge – which is free indirect style itself – between them simultaneously closes the gap and draws attention to its distance.[31]

Though I would prefer the term narrator to author, Wood makes an important point here. One of the interesting things about free indirect discourse is that narrators can generate a degree of uncertainty about the source of ideas and opinions; they can simultaneously assert and qualify ideas; to put it another way, narrators can offset the kind of authoritative, absolutist voice that has been deemed an unacceptable facet of omniscient narration. As Rimmon-Kenan says, free indirect discourse potentially 'dramatises the problematic relationship between any utterance and its origin'; which is to say that free indirect discourse responds to the uncertainty associated with words and their relationship with reality. At the same

---

[31] James Wood, *How Fiction Works* (London: Vintage, 2009) p.11

time, free indirect discourse 'enhances the bivocality or polyvocality of the text by bringing into play a plurality of speakers and attitudes' (*Narrative Fiction*, p.113); by this Rimmon-Kenan means that texts can juxtapose a multiplicity of voices, and the attitudes and values associated with those voices, in a non-hierarchical way, allowing them to mingle freely in the narrative world. This is a significant function of fiction and one of the reasons why it might be considered such an important art form. It is this facet of fiction that the novelist Carlos Fuentes had in mind when he referred to the novel as:

> ... the privileged arena where languages in conflict can meet, bringing together, in tension and dialogue, not only opposing characters, but also different historical ages, social levels, civilisation and other, dawning realities of human life. In the novel, realities that are normally separated can meet, establishing a dialogic encounter, a meeting with the other.[32]

Because conflict is fundamental to the human experience, it is important to have a space where oppositional ideas can be expressed and interrogated in an even-handed way. Arguably, this cannot happen in novels where all voices are subordinate to, and controlled by, a narrator, but it *can* happen in a narrative environment which allows parity between all voices; free indirect discourse can facilitate this because neither the narrator's voice nor the character's voice

---

[32] Carlos Fuentes 'Worlds Apart', the *Guardian*, 24 February 1989; reprinted in *The Rushdie File* eds. Lisa Appignanesi and Sara Maitland (London: Fourth Estate, 1989) pp.245-48.

is privileged. At the beginning it was suggested that fiction can be liberating because it allows people to address things that would be difficult to tackle in non-fiction, and fiction's capacity to create a space for non-hierarchical debate is one of the reasons why this is the case: authors, via their narrators, can juxtapose opinions and values without necessarily being associated with any position themselves.

Some writers explore the possibility of equality among voices in other ways too. Writers such as James Joyce, or more recently, Cormac McCarthy, Roddy Doyle and Irvine Welsh introduce their characters' direct speech with a dash rather than quotation marks, and this can have interesting effects. For instance, here is an exchange from the opening of Welsh's *Trainspotting* where the first-person narrator, Renton, and his friend Sick Boy are watching a Jean-Claude Van Damme video:

> As it happens in such movies, they started oaf wi an obligatory dramatic opening. Then the next phase ay the picture involved building up the tension through introducing the dastardly villain and sticking the weak plot thegither. Any minute now though, auld Jean-Claude's ready tae git doon tae some serious swedgin.
> – Rents. Ah've goat tae see Mother Superior, Sick Boy gasped, shaking his heid.
> – Aw, ah sais. Ah wanted the radge tae jist fuck off ootay ma visage, tae go oan his ain, n jist leave us wi Jean-Claude. Oan the other hand, ah'd be gitting sick tae before long, and if that cunt went n scored, he'd haud oot oan us. They call urn Sick Boy, no because he's eywis sick wi junk withdrawal, but because he's just one sick cunt.

> – Let's fuckin go, he snapped desperately.
> – Haud oan a second.[33]

The dialogue seems less cut off from the narrator's speech than in conventional quotation, partly because the dashes appear less visually intrusive than quotation marks. Also, Renton speaks to the reader with the same voice that he uses to address his friends, which arguably augments our sense of his authenticity as a narrator, and our impression that he is confiding in us. This impression is compounded by the fact that his voice is in dialect, which he does not feel the need to adjust when addressing the reader. It is quite rare in novels for a primary narrator to use dialect: if dialect is used at all, it's mostly confined to the characters' speech. Certainly, it is unusual for the thoughts of such characters to be revealed via dialect, and this too has an interesting effect: it reminds us that such characters do indeed possess complex interior lives, comparable to our own.

Elsewhere in the novel the narrative switches to the third person, and on these occasions the narrator's voice employs Standard English:

> Spud and Renton were sitting in a pub in the Royal Mile. The pub aimed at an American theme-bar but not too accurately; it was a madhouse of assorted bric-à-brac.
> – Fuckin weird man though, likesay, you n me gittin sent fir the same joab, ken? Spud said, slurping at his Guinness.

---

[33] Irvine Welsh, *Trainspotting* (London: Minerva, 1996; first published, 1993) p.3. Future references will be made to this edition.

> – Fuckin disaster fir me mate. Ah'm no wantin the fuckin joab. It's be a fuckin nightmare. Renton shook his head.
> – Yeah, ah'm likesay happy steyin oan the rock n roll the now man, ken? (p.62)

It might be said that the decision not to bracket off the quoted speech is even more important here because to do so might be to imply a hierarchy between standard and colloquial voices, privileging the former over the latter. The dashes allow the voices to exist on a more equal footing – visually at least they seem to occupy the same level. This has potential ideological implications in *Trainspotting* given the novel's frequent references to Scotland's history of political subordination to England: Standard English carries with it a patina of authority and superiority which the novel seeks to qualify.

Dialogue and Creative Writing

Dialogue is a staple of most fiction, and creative writers use it for a variety of reasons. As suggested earlier, dialogue can offer an effective way of delineating characters via indirect presentation, revealing them through the manner and the content of their speech. For instance, a lot can be learned about Spud and Renton in the dialogue from *Trainspotting* cited above: details of their culture, social class, and attitude to life are all discernible to some extent. Dialogue can also be used to advance the plot, of course, offering a succinct method of communicating information whilst at the same time adding immediacy to the narrative. Dialogue adjusts the pace of a story too – when a scene is dramatised the story potentially slows down to real time, and such shifts in tempo offer a way manipulating the speed at which the story unfolds.

Novice creative writers often have a problem with dialogue partly because it looks and feels simple to write, and hence they put less effort into it than they should. It is very easy to write too much of it; with many people learning to write is about learning what to leave out and this is particularly true of dialogue. As in all creative writing, writers should strive only to include significant detail. Problems also occur when writers try to construct what they consider to be 'realistic' conversation. Fictional dialogue tends to be more convincing when it gives the impression of realism, without trying to scrupulously emulate real-life – real-life dialogues are mostly bloated and boring; in the main, fictional dialogue should be employed only to serve the functions mentioned above: if it doesn't serve a function then it should not be there. Certainly there needs to be something at issue in any verbal exchanges the characters have – few things detract from the force of a story more quickly than empty dialogue. Also, it is worth remembering that the unsaid can be as communicative as what is on the page; sub-text is very often important in fiction, and it is good to cultivate the ability to use dialogue to convey a character's unspoken attitudes and beliefs. It is also usually desirable to contextualise dialogue, locating verbal exchanges in a world that readers can visualise, and not allowing them to lose sight of that world. Many writers are careful to intersperse dialogue with references to the physical environment of the characters who are speaking in order to effectively ground it; if they don't they risk readers losing track of the 'where, when and why' of a scene, and the characters can resemble disembodied voices, detached from the context that gives them meaning.

Conclusion: Creating Critical and Fictional Narratives

In her book *Reading like a Writer* (2006),[34] the novelist and critic Francine Prose says, 'Like most – maybe all – writers I learned to write by writing and, by example, by reading books.' The best possible advice one writer can give another is to write and read as much as possible. Writing narratives of any kind is a craft, and those who seek to create them need to practice their craft by writing and, perhaps more importantly, by rewriting. Whether writing criticism or fiction, the process is likely to involve producing drafts, and then reworking them. Many fledgling writers fail to see the importance of this and are too eager to view a narrative as finished. Think of redrafting as an inevitable part of the writing process. It is often a very good idea to produce a draft and then put it aside for a while before redrafting: this way it is possible to achieve a degree of detachment from the text, and a clearer,

---

[34] Francine Prose, *Reading Like a Writer* (New York: HarperCollins, 2006) p.2

more objective perspective than is possible when one is immersed in the writing process.

Reading is just as important as writing. It is impossible to develop proficiency either as a literary critic or as a fiction writer without studying the work of other writers. Explore the techniques and possibilities of literary criticism by reading published literary criticism: read it with a view to assessing how other critics use the concepts and terminology introduced in this book; likewise, learn how to write narrative fiction by studying how other people do it. This should be obvious, but it doesn't always appear to be. It is crucial to appreciate the relationship between reading and writing, and to understand that good critics read good criticism, and good fiction writers read good fiction. When reading as a writer, try to read actively rather than passively: for literary critics this means noting how other critics construct arguments, how they utilise theory, and critical vocabulary. For creative writers it means thinking about the form the story takes, how it is structured, who tells it, how the characters are delineated, what they say and how they say it. Given that narratives don't write themselves, these are all choices that the writer has had to make: why have they made them? How do they contribute to the import of the narrative? How do they influence the way you interpret or evaluate it? Reading actively can also mean taking issue with a text – developing writers are often far too respectful of published narrative. Just because a piece of work is in print doesn't make it true or necessarily valuable. When reading criticism, be on the lookout for specious arguments: try to identify the central thesis in an argument, and determine whether it is fully supported with evidence, or consistent with theory: are there any alternative ways to view the narrative in question? Similarly, it is useful for creative writers to think as editors: consider potential ways of improving the narrative in terms of increasing the tension in the story, for instance, or the credibility of the fictional world. Reading actively means reading everyone's work as an editor might read it.

The French poet and critic Paul Valéry once said that 'A poem is never finished, only abandoned'[35], and while this might suggest a degree of obsessiveness, it is applicable to any activity that involves craft: the construction of narrative included.

---

[35] Quoted in Michael Krausz, Denis Dutton, and Karen Bardsley (eds.) *The Idea of Creativity* (Leiden: Koninklijke Brill NV, 2009) p.107

Bibliography

Books on Narrative

Bal, Mieke *Narratology: Introduction to the Theory of Narrative* (Toronto: University of Toronto Press, 2009). This was first published in the mid-eighties and is now in its third edition. It is a useful introduction to narrative poetics and theory from a structuralist perspective, covering such ground as types and levels of narration, story ordering, character construction, and time and space in narrative. The approach is rather dry, but the third edition is more accessible than the first as the author has spent time untangling some of the complex and jargon-laden passages that marred the latter.

Barthes, Roland *S/Z* (New York: Hill and Wang, 1975). This is Barthes's ground-breaking analysis of Balzac's novella, *Sarrasine*. He identifies five 'codes' that in combination could be said to constitute this text and the way[s] it signifies; he stresses the irreducible plurality of the text: the extent to which the codes are not fixed, but dependent on context and individual interpretation. The book takes a structuralist approach, but it is generally considered to be one of the first important poststructuralist works in its focus on the fluidity and subjective production of meaning.

Booker, Christopher *The Seven Basic Plots: Why We Tell Stories* (London: Continuum, 2004). This book is aimed at the popular market, and it has been criticised for its generalisations and occasionally eccentric interpretations of texts, but the case for basic plots is made with eloquence, conviction, and with reference to a huge amount of examples.

Booth, Wayne C. *The Rhetoric of Fiction* (Chicago: The University of Chicago Press, 1961). A modern classic of its kind, even though his moralising approach to writing has been criticised; he is particularly good on perspective and narrative typology.

Cohan, Steven and Shires, Linda M. *Telling Stories: A Theoretical Analysis of Narrative Fiction* (London: Routledge, 1988). A book addressing narratives of various kinds (film, fiction, comics and advertising), making the point that they can only be understood in relation to their cultural context. It has a useful chapter on narrative structure, and a particularly worthwhile reading of *Pride and Prejudice* as a sequence of story events.

Forster, E.M. *Aspects of the Novel* (London: Penguin Classics, 2005; originally published, 1927). This is a collection of lectures given by Forster at Cambridge in the 1920s. It is still widely cited, and his distinction between round and flat characters has been particularly enduring.

Lodge, David *The Art of Fiction* (London: Penguin, 1992). A collection of short articles on various aspects of fiction writing produced for the *Independent on Sunday* in the early 1990s. The fact they are written for a lay audience makes them particularly accessible. It includes pieces on, among other things, suspense, point of view, stream of consciousness, character, intertextuality, showing and telling, and metafiction. In each case, the topic is illustrated with reference to an extract from a work of fiction.

Propp, Vladímir *Morphology of the Folktale* (University of Texas Press, 1968; originally published, 1928). A seminal work on plot structure that influenced many subsequent approaches to the topic.

Messent, Peter *New Readings of the American Novel: Narrative Theory and Its Application* (London: MacMillan, 1990). A book that applies narrative theory to a number of classic American novels. Among other things it covers character construction in Hemingway's *The Sun Also Rises*, and Barthesian readings of Henry James's *The Portrait of a Lady*, and Edith Wharton's *The House of Mirth*. Good for developing a sense of how narratological concepts can be applied to fiction.

Rimmon-Kenan, Shlomith *Narrative Fiction: Contemporary Poetics* (London: Methuen, 1983). This is a succinct book on narrative mechanics which covers important ground, making reference to the various significant contributors to narratology up to the early 1980s. Organised in a sensible way around key themes of story, text, and narration, it remains one of the best introductions to the field.

Todorov, Tzvetan *The Poetics of Prose* (Oxford: Blackwell, 1977). One of several books by Todorov on narrative; this one focuses on such issues as narrative grammar, the significance of ellipses and absences in narrative, with particular reference to the work of Henry James.

Wood, James *How Fiction Works* (London: Vintage, 2009). This very readable book tackles various aspects of fictional narrative. It includes a useful discussion of free indirect discourse, and a very good section on the influence of Gustave Flaubert on modern narrative technique, particularly regarding the author's ability to adopt a seemingly objective narrative perspective in his work.

Useful Books for Creative Writers

Cox, Ailsa *Writing Short Stories* (London: Routledge, 2005). This is one of the best books for prospective short story writers. It is an intelligent account of the discipline, covering important ground on plotting stories, together with insightful discussions of how humour, fantasy, epiphany, and romance take shape in short fiction.

Earnshaw, Steven ed. *The Handbook of Creative Writing* (Edinburgh: Edinburgh University Press, 2007). This is a collection of articles on various aspects of creative writing; it contains a large section on the craft of writing with particular reference to writing novels, humour, historical fiction, and writing for children.

Prose, Francine *Reading Like a Writer* (New York: HarperCollins, 2006). In this excellent book the author shares her reading life and talks about the relationship between reading and writing as she sees it. It contains lots of examples of good practise on issues like sentence construction, narration, characterisation and dialogue.

Watts, Nigel *Writing a Novel* (London: Hodder and Stoughton, 2003). First published in 1996, this is a book in the Teach Yourself series which offers lots of practical advice on producing a novel. It is particularly good on plotting, but it also includes useful chapters on characterisation and dialogue.

Fictional Narratives Mentioned

Jane Austen, *Pride and Prejudice* (1813)

Iain Banks, *Complicity* (2000)

John Barth, 'Lost in the Funhouse' (1968)

Charlotte Brontë, *Jane Eyre* (1847)

Emily Brontë, *Wuthering Heights* (1847)

Fredric Brown, 'Knock', from *Thrilling Wonder Stories*, December 1948.

Lewis Carroll, *Alice's Adventures in Wonderland* (1865)

Angela Carter, *Wise Children* (1991)

Joseph Conrad, *Heart of Darkness* (1899)

Charles Dickens, *A Christmas Carol* (1843)

——————— *Great Expectations* (1861)

George Eliot, *Middlemarch* (1874)

Bret Easton Ellis, *American Psycho* (1991)

William Faulkner, 'Barn Burning' in *Selected Short Stories of William Faulkner* (1961)

Joshua Ferris, *Then We Came To The End* (2007)

Henry Fielding, *Tom Jones* (1749)

F. Scott Fitzgerald, *The Great Gatsby* (1925)

Charles Frazier, *Cold Mountain* (1997)

Elizabeth Gaskell, *North and South* (1854)

Mark Haddon, *The Curious Incident of the Dog in the Night-Time* (2003)

Ernest Hemingway, 'The Killers' in *The Complete Short Stories of Ernest Hemingway* (1987)

Laura Hird, *Born Free* (1999)

Khaled Hosseini, *The Kite Runner* (2003)

Homer, *The Odyssey* (700 BC)

James Joyce, *Dubliners* (1914)

―――――― *A Portrait of the Artist as a Young Man* (1916)

―――――― *Ulysses* (1922)

Andrea Levi, *Small Island* (2004)

David Lodge, *Nice Work* (1988)

David Nicholls, *One Day* (2009)

Catherine O'Flynn, *What Was Lost* (2007)

Dan Rhodes, 'Laughing', from *Anthropology: And a Hundred Other Stories* (2005)

Philip Roth, *The Counterlife* (1986)

―――――― *The Human Stain* (2000)

J.D. Salinger, *Catcher in the Rye* (1951)

Laurence Sterne, *Tristram Shandy* (1767)

Irvine Welsh, *Trainspotting* (1993)

H.G. Wells, *The Time Machine* (1895)

Oscar Wilde, *The Picture of Dorian Grey* (1890)

STORY
THE HEART OF THE MATTER

Maggie Butt (editor)

978-1-871551-93-8
184pp (pbk)

What can't we get enough of? Food? Sex? Alcohol? Stories? We devour hundreds of stories every day in television news, magazines, novels, movies, jokes, plays, newspapers, and we never get tired of them. Stories always leave us hungry for more.

In this book, 15 established writers explore their own practice and ideas about storymaking. These novelists, journalists, poets, screenwriters, playwrights, documentary makers, oral storytellers and stand-up comics are also leading academics in Creative Writing and Journalism in UK universities. What do they have in common? Story.

Their examinations of storymaking shed new light on what different forms, media and genres have in common. These writers don't tell you how to write a play, or novel or poem, but they offer personal insights which are the fruit of years of experience. They share some of the ways to create that all-important connection between the idea and the audience – how to make the magic happen.

THE AUTHOR, THE BOOK & THE READER

Robert Giddings

987-1-871551-01-3
240pp (pbk)

In this book Robert Giddings explores the literary nexus – the interdependence always existing between writers and their readers through the production and distribution of books. Drawing upon information and insights from the disciplines of history, sociology and politics, as well as media studies and literary criticism, he illuminates the fascinating variation in the ways in which authors have tackled the challenge of truth and storytelling. The eight authors chosen to illustate this theme range from Samuel Johnson in the 18th century to John le Carré in the 20th and all are studied in the cultural context of their time with an emphasis upon the channels of communication and the available technology of printing and publishing. The topic of the how and the why of writing is here treated in a robust and original way and will be of interest to all those with a love of literature in English.

POETRY MASTERCLASS

John Greening

978-1-906075-58-3
142pp (pbk)

John Greening's *Poetry Masterclass* is more than just a reference book, although you will find here an extensive glossary of technical terms and verse forms, together with book recommendations and even a brief history of poetry in English. It is also a supremely practical handbook, including well over a hundred creative writing ideas for teachers, students and fledgling poets, with chapters on how to teach a poem, read a poem, write a poem ... Above all, this is a very personal guide by an experienced teacher and established poet: a practitioner offering personal, hands-on advice and demonstrations of technique, much as a performer might during a musical masterclass.

A GUIDE TO GOOD WRITTEN ENGLISH

Vera Hughes

978-1-906075-70-5
156pp (pbk)

If you want to be sure that your written English is correct and up-to-date, this book is for you. The author's aim is to help you remember the basic rules of spelling, grammar and punctuation. The book teaches the clear, accurate English required by the business, academic and office world, coaching in acceptable current usage and making the rules easier to remember.

You can use this book in three ways:

- Work through it from the beginning if you want to improve your skills all round;

- Check specific points – apostrophes or colons, for example – by referring to the relevant sections; and

- Use any of the 48 Practice Sessions as revision.

The extensive Exercise and Practice sections include topics such as IT, a radio script, a letter of condolence and a speech about litter in the park, as well as the normal letters, email and reports found in any business.

To find out more about these and other titles visit
www.greenex.co.uk